T0285844

IF WALLS COULD TALK

THE HIGH PRICE OF A PICTURE-PERFECT FAMILY

SANDEE JO CROCKER

WITH KEN ABRAHAM

Forefront
BOOKS

Published by Forefront Books, Nashville, Tennessee.
Distributed by Simon & Schuster.

Library of Congress Control Number: 2024911800

Print ISBN: 978-1-63763-226-0
E-book ISBN: 978-1-63763-227-7

Cover Design by Studiogearbox
Interior Design by Bill Kersey, KerseyGraphics

Printed in the United States of America

This book is dedicated to anyone who has ever suffered at the hands of an abusive partner, and to their family.

A Note from Sandee Jo

Several people have asked me why I would be willing to tell this story now. Why share such intimate, and sometimes humiliating, details that have not been revealed publicly before this time? What do I hope to gain?

The answer is simple: I want to help.

I want those who are currently trapped in abusive situations to know they are not alone. I want them to be able to relate to my story and feel a deep connection. Then I want them to feel empowered to follow my advice and get out. If hindsight is 20/20, I'm hoping my hindsight enables them to see their situation with absolute clarity.

Perhaps there are others who are beginning relationships, and after reading my book, they will find themselves far more equipped to spot early warning signs of abuse.

Many others may find themselves in proximity to abuse. It is my hope they'll be better informed of the prevalence of partner abuse, and how easily it can exist right under their unsuspecting noses. Perhaps these individuals will become more suspecting, aware, and able to become a part of an army of motivated, proactive advocates for those suffering from partner abuse.

CONTENTS

Foreword

Walls don't talk. They never have and never will. Some victims of partner abuse talk about their experiences, but the fact is that the vast majority never do. Fear, embarrassment, shame, lack of time, lack of financial means, and a host of other factors discourage or prevent people from telling the stories that ought to be told. Those who do muster the courage and resources to tell, deserve so much credit. There have been plenty of nights over the last few years that I've had to awaken Sandee Jo out of her nightmares, and I worried that she might quit. However, I'm not sure the thought of quitting ever got to first base in her mind. Once she caught the vision of helping others through her story, she relentlessly pursued the completion of this book, and I am so very proud of her daytime work of writing and her nighttime work in pushing through those nightmares.

It may be difficult to find any subject that has more impact on our families, our communities, our churches, our children, our society, on future generations, and on our world, yet is talked about so little. Not just from our pulpits, from where you might expect it to be addressed, but from television talk shows, news broadcasts, magazine articles, and books—except for the rare exception you're about to read.

The pattern is remarkably consistent. Some gal gets involved with a guy who has never learned to control his anger, jealousy, greed, or other evil impulses. He starts out so nice. Love, of course, is impatient and fails to allow time for a person's true self to be revealed and the gloss to fade to the real man. Even when there are a few signs, love is blind and thus blurs the ability to see anything but the tip of the proverbial iceberg. The next thing you know, they move in together or get married or have a baby together, any of which can make it far more difficult to break away. Once an abuser feels that his partner's departure is difficult, the trap is set. He then gets comfortable allowing his true nature to come out unbridled. Soon enough, things escalate, and another sad statistic becomes reality. Wouldn't it be great if at the end of an occasional one of these stories, we'd learn how to spot the early signs of an abuser? Why not educate and equip women and girls with the advice and tools that may enable them to get out or, better yet, never get into this situation in the first place.

It's not unusual that the early warning signs of abuse are ignored or assigned an offsetting lie, such as, "Well, everybody has a bad day now and then" or, "When I get him to church and he gets saved or confirmed, his rough edges will disappear," or, "When we have kids, the kids will soften him and he'll be nice then." By the time you've read this book, those lies and a thousand like them will be replaced with truth. Hopefully reading this book will raise your awareness, and you'll begin to look for ways to be proactive. Get involved in a local shelter, attend a fundraiser, cook a meal for a single mom who may have found the courage to leave an abusive situation, volunteer at your local church if they have any related programs, and repost social media stories when they highlight the problem or a partial solution. The key to improvement on any front is awareness and you can be a part of that.

The gripping firsthand account you're about to read stretches the imagination. It will increase your awarenesses as to how an abuser maintains control over the abused and the pattern of escalation. Armed with your fresh perspective, you'll be better equipped to identify abusers and help your loved ones steer clear or break free of such a person. Unlike many of the stories you may have heard on television shows, this one has a happier ending.

James Crocker, September, 2024

CHAPTER I

Incriminating Evidence

How could I have let this happen? I asked myself repeatedly. I had long ago decided that I could survive almost anything, as long as I kept my children safe from their father's irrational violent outbursts. Now my worst fears had happened. The man from whom I had endured eighteen years of unspeakable abuse lay in our bed, dead from a gunshot wound to the head. I had desperately sought to prevent this horror so my children would not be hurt. Now, here I was, sitting in a strange car, while three of my children were sequestered at our neighbors' home. My seventeen-year-old son rode alone in a separate squad car, on the way to the police station for questioning.

How could I have let this happen? I asked myself over and over again.

Calling the police was something I had wanted to do for a long time, but I had been too afraid. I had tried once before and had nearly gotten killed. That day, when the police pulled down our lane, my husband hid behind our bedroom door with a loaded rifle, threatening to kill them, then me, and himself. I had plenty of reasons to believe he would carry out his threats. So I told the officers that the 911 call must have been an accident, and though they may not have believed me, they left.

Years later I would finally make another 911 call—well, to be precise, my friend would do it for me—and when she dialed 911, she didn't hang up.

Earlier that evening, I had looked at my son Tommy (known to our family and friends as "Bubba," to avoid confusion with his dad and grandfather, also named Thomas).

"We have to call the police," I said to him.

Bubba, who still held the rifle with which he had killed his father, nodded in understanding.

For some reason, I called my neighbor Patsy Wisdom first. She came immediately and took the kids and me to her home, and we called the police from there. This time I was not calling to report my husband's profane verbal threats—that he was going to kill me or one of our children—or to file a complaint that he had been punching me, kicking me, choking me, or dragging me by my hair from one room to another. I was not calling to report him chopping up our furniture with a chain saw in the middle of the dining room, heaving a stove through the window, or smashing glass all over our kitchen. No, I had not called to report his awful physical and emotional abuse of our family.

Patsy contacted the police to tell them my husband was dead— and that my seventeen-year-old son had shot him in the head with a .22 caliber rifle.

Just before we disconnected the call with the 911 operator, a couple of police cruisers arrived at Patsy's home. I later learned that others had raced to our house, sirens wailing, red and blue lights flashing, casting eerie images against the backdrop of trees surrounding our property in the dark Tennessee evening. Several officers had bounded out of the vehicles and, with guns raised, had gingerly stepped inside the house. One policeman soon came back outside and holstered his gun, nodding his head toward his partners.

Waiting with Patsy and my children, I wasn't too worried. Surely the officers would ask us some questions while the investigators noted the bullet holes in the walls of our home and in the driveway. I was confident that they would allow us to tell our story when they found the arsenal of weapons my husband, Tommy, had scattered all around our home—in the living room, the bedroom, even above the tiles in the dropped ceiling of the house. No doubt they'd find the large jugs of inexpensive whiskey from which he had been drinking since early that morning, mixing booze with prescription medications intended to calm his erratic, bipolar behavior. They'd discover the pickax Tommy had wielded in his strong hands, brandishing it dangerously at our son, Bubba, and yelling, "I'm going to kill you! I'm going to split your head wide open like a melon!" Even in the dark, surely they'd stumble upon the broken pieces of cinder blocks and bricks that, in his drunken stupor, Tommy had hurled at our boy.

Finally, I could tell somebody what my four children and I had endured for so long. My two boys—Bubba, seventeen, and Timmy, fifteen—and two girls—Tonie Jo, thirteen, and Tayler Jewell, only nine years of age—had witnessed their father doing unspeakable, despicable things to me, and had lived in fear all of their lives. I had longed to tell the police so many times but hadn't dared. Tommy had repeatedly warned me against doing so. "I'll never spend a day in prison," he boasted. "The cops will never take me alive."

Now I *wanted* to tell the authorities. I had held it all inside me for so long.

The officers wrote down some brief notes on a clipboard after talking to Bubba, me, and our neighbor.

"We'll need you and your son to come down to the station, ma'am," one of the policemen said to me. He seemed polite and respectful, almost sympathetic.

"Okay," I mumbled. "Bubba, let's go with them." I nodded toward the officers. I assumed Bubba and I could ride together, so we started toward Patsy's car.

"No, ma'am," the officer said. "We'll need your son to come with us in our car. One of your friends can drive you, and you can follow behind us."

I felt numb. I was still in a daze and could barely comprehend his words, but our friends led me toward a car. Then one of the officers pulled Bubba's hands together and clapped handcuffs onto them. He placed a hand on Bubba's head and guided him into the back seat of the cruiser. I stared in disbelief at the sight of my son's expressionless face, barely visible through the back window of the police car.

When we arrived at the police station, the officers escorted us inside. "Right this way, ma'am," an officer said, leading me toward a room down the hall with the door already open. A female officer accompanied my neighbors and me in that direction, as another officer separated Bubba from us and led him to an interrogation room all by himself.

Still, I wasn't worried. Although I was shaken by the events of the day and self-conscious about talking with the police, I no longer had an overwhelming sense of dread. I wasn't afraid of retaliation or consequences for speaking up and telling the truth. No longer was I concerned about Tommy's family or mine finding out, or more likely, confirming what they already suspected. "I'll answer any questions you have," I told the officers.

Maybe because I had been operating on such an intense, high level of fear and anxiety all day long, it felt good to sit safely and calm down a bit. Oddly, my emotions bounced back and forth between grief and relief. I was terribly sad that Tommy was dead. He was my husband, after all—the man who had swept me off my feet when I was still a teenager, the man with whom I had brought four beautiful children into the world. On the other hand, he was the monster who had terrorized me for eighteen and a half years, not to mention the fear he inflicted upon our family members. So I felt a mishmash of emotions as I sat waiting for the Lawrenceburg police officers to do their work.

Lawrenceburg, Tennessee, was a friendly community of approximately ten thousand residents (nearly double that today), located about ninety miles south of Nashville. It had been the hometown of Davy Crockett, the American folk hero and frontiersman known for his expertise in killing bears with a trusty long-barreled, .40 caliber flintlock rifle he affectionately referred to as Old Betsy. Crockett died at the Alamo in 1836, but his spirit lived on in Lawrenceburg, where his small log home could still be viewed when our family moved nearby in 2005.

Although many residents in the area owned guns, our crime rate was low, so we didn't need a large police force. Murder investigations in our area were rare.

Consequently, I didn't expect matters to move quickly but assumed the officers would soon have the information they needed. Then Bubba, our friends, and I could all return home together. I simply took it for granted that the authorities would believe my account of the day. I had no reason to lie or exaggerate the details.

But as the night wore on and the officers continued to ask me questions—most of which I had already answered several times—a stunning realization dawned on me: *They don't believe me. They don't trust that I'm telling them the truth!* That possibility had not even occurred to me.

So I told the awful story all over again, everything I could remember, beginning from early in the morning until the moment the police cars pulled down our lane. As gut-wrenching as the day had been, and as heartrending as it was to rehash the details, I was relieved to be alive to speak about it. I repeated the account again… and again.

As I sat in the interrogation room, my body aching and my head pounding, one of the officers pointed at the washed-out gray sweatsuit with red lettering I was wearing. "Where did that blood on your clothing come from?" he asked.

For the first time, I noticed blood spatter in various spots on my sweatsuit and on my body. The day had been such a blur, I hadn't taken time to consider my own injuries. My eyes followed the officer's gaze as we both focused on the dried blood on my hands. I had not washed or changed my clothing prior to the arrival of the police at our house, so I still looked exactly as I had the moment Bubba told me, "Mom, I shot Dad."

"Where did that blood come from?" the officer probed. His voice sounded a bit testier now. "Tell me precisely how it got there."

"I…I'm not sure," I answered, raising and turning my hands so I could see better where all the blood was located. "I don't really know for sure…" My voice trailed off.

"You don't know," the female officer repeated brusquely.

"I'm not sure. There was so much struggling…for several hours…" I knew I was being vague, but I honestly had no clue when or how I had gotten the blood on me. "We fought on and off, all day long…"

The officer crossed her arms over her chest and glared at me silently.

I did a mental check of my body. My throat hurt where I could still feel Tommy's strong hands squeezing around my neck, choking me. No doubt there were red marks on my neck and shoulders. My entire body throbbed and ached from head to toe, but I didn't see any visible cuts or lacerations or feel any moist areas where I might be bleeding. I was certain I'd find plenty of black, blue, and purple blotches on my body by morning. I always did after one of Tommy's beatings.

Then suddenly it came to me. I saw an image in my mind of Tommy smashing cement blocks against each other, breaking cinder blocks with his bare hands and hurling the pieces in the direction of our son's head. Although his hands were rugged and calloused from working with wood, the rough cinder block had sliced Tommy's fingers—and when he shoved me to the ground or pushed me off him as I tried to protect Bubba, his blood had probably splashed onto me.

When I realized the blood on my clothes had to be from Tommy, I looked up at the police officers and blurted, "I'm fine! This is my husband's blood."

I had naïvely assumed the police were concerned about my well-being, worried I might be injured. I had not even considered that they might be questioning my innocence. Nor had I realized that by explaining the blood on my body and clothes as Tommy's, I was potentially incriminating myself!

That information provided fresh impetus to the interrogators, who immediately fired more questions at me. "How did his blood get on your clothes? Where were you and what were you doing to get his blood all over your hands?"

My head pounded like a hammer on a steel anvil, and my words slurred as my voice barely exited my parched throat. "I don't know. We fought...so much...Bubba ran...I tried to stop his dad by tackling him..."

None of my answers made much sense to the officers. In fact, one of the female officers seemed irritated by my responses. She didn't even pretend to hide her disgust with me, as though she thought I was hedging, hiding something sinister, or making up the entire story.

After more questions, one of my friends who had accompanied me recognized my precarious position, even if I did not. She leaned over and gently tapped me on the arm. "Sandee Jo," she spoke quietly. "Maybe you should get a lawyer before you say anything else."

"What?" I looked back at her in astonishment. "A lawyer? Why? Who, me? Why would I need a lawyer?"

My friend lightly gripped my arm and nodded.

For the first time all evening it struck me that, to the arresting officers, I looked guilty—regardless of how innocent I was, or how victimized I'd been by my husband once again, or how Bubba had admitted to pulling the trigger.

With the officers' permission, my friends helped me out of the police station. Bubba, the officers had informed me, had to stay. "Don't worry, ma'am," the polite officer said. "He'll be fine. He's not going to jail. Because of his age, he'll be going to a juvenile detention center for a few days till we sort things out."

I nodded weakly. I assumed the police had more to investigate as they gathered pictures in the daylight and interviewed the neighbors. I knew in my heart that the truth was obvious, and the officers would surely see it. I simply trusted everyone involved. I had no idea that Bubba faced first-degree murder charges with the possibility of years in prison—and I might too.

My neighbors offered to let my three younger children and me stay with them for the night, but first my friends Gail Dixon and Melissa Brazier drove me back to the house. Our entire property was now taped off. It was considered a crime scene and investigators were still working, but the police allowed us inside the house so I could gather some clean clothing and personal items. I shuddered as I walked down the same hallway toward our bedroom—my bedroom now—where only a few hours earlier I had been frantic with fear, terrified that we were all going to die that day.

My friends closed ranks tightly around me, helping to lead me down the hall as the recent memories flooded through my mind. *Oh, God, how could this have happened? Tommy and I were so in love. How did we ever get to this awful place in our lives?*

CHAPTER 2

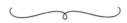

Growing Pains
and Palm Trees

Gently swaying palm trees, white sand beaches, and blue bay water surrounded me in the heart of Tampa, Florida, where I grew up. I developed a spunky personality early on. I was not a wimpy, wallflower type of woman who would tolerate being abused by a man. Neither were the women in my family. Actually, they were quite the opposite.

My grandparents moved from Michigan to Tampa when my mom was only three years old. Soon after their extended family, including most of the aunts and uncles, joined my grandparents in Tampa as well.

My mom, Sandy, was the oldest of four girls. She had long, dark hair, and she and her sisters were all beautiful. They were trendy and loved fashionable clothes. At sixteen, my mom met and married a man who was taking correspondence courses from Trevecca University in Nashville and was planning to be a missionary. But on my mom's seventeenth birthday, he was robbed, shot, and killed while working at a Florida convenience store. He and Mom had been married little more than six months when the attack took place. Not surprisingly, her sadness soon turned into disillusionment with God. Her questions ran the gamut from, "How could You let this happen?" to "Do You not love us? Didn't You call him to be a missionary?" to "God, don't You care?"

Later she remarried—this time to my father. Together they had two children, my brother, Billy, and me. Billy was barely a year old when I was born. My parents named me Sandee Jo—Sandee after my mom, and Joanne after my grandma on Mom's side of the family, my nana.

Mom had been raised in a strict Christian home, but Dad didn't hold such a high view of marriage. He was unfaithful to Mom, and his numerous sexual affairs caused their marriage to fall apart. Reeling from the hurt, Mom wandered further away from God after our dad cheated on her. It would be years before Mom found the courage to trust in a good God again.

For most of my childhood, she always had a boyfriend—and occasionally, a husband. During this time, Mom started drinking heavily and didn't stop for years.

Eventually she remarried, and with the help of her husband, Bill, overcame her dependence on alcohol. As I write these words, Mom has been sober for more than thirteen years.

Divorce became a common occurrence in my family. Both my mom and my dad married five times. Other close relatives also divorced. More than anything, I did not want that to happen to me.

During the time I attended sixth through eighth grades, we lived in Summit West Apartments on Fowler Avenue. My friend Roxie and I roller-skated in the streets. I walked to school and rode my bike to the mall, and our neighborhood was relatively safe.

But one of Mom's long-term boyfriends, Prince, no relation to the music artist, was a drug dealer. On one occasion, he took our family to Belize for a fun-filled monthlong vacation. While there we visited the ancient Mayan ruins. No doubt, he also purchased marijuana and other illegal substances while we were there. Ironically, my future husband, Tommy, was there around that time with his family, serving on a Christian mission trip. We didn't meet then, but it was an interesting topic of conversation in future years.

One night, several years after we returned from Central America, Mom had been drinking again and said matter-of-factly to her current boyfriend, "Well, I killed him."

The boyfriend said nothing in response.

I was in bed, but I heard Mom's words. "What?" I cried.

"I killed him," Mom repeated loudly. "I stabbed Prince."

Sure enough, Mom had stabbed Prince in the leg above the knee with a large butcher knife. I thought for sure that Prince was dead, and I was sad because I loved him. I was in sixth grade at the time, and the next morning, I got up and went to school as though nothing had happened. But when I came home, police cars had surrounded our apartment building.

Mom's sister, my Aunt Susie, and Uncle Darrell were there too, and the police said that Billy and I were to stay with them for a few days.

Fortunately for us, Prince refused to press charges against Mom. Apparently, when he arrived at the hospital, the doctors and the police asked him, "Who did this to you?"

He covered for Mom and said, "I did it to myself. It was an accident."

They knew my mom had done it, but she was never formally charged.

Prince never stopped loving Mom, and years later on his deathbed, he asked for her to come to him. His girlfriend at the time even called Mom and said, "He's dying and is asking to see you."

Mom decided not to go.

I never saw Prince again.

Mom was quick to admit her mistakes. But I always knew she loved me, and I loved her with all my heart. I enjoyed being with her, although we had limited time together because she worked so much. Throughout my early teenage years, Mom worked as a paramedic, so she always had a job and always paid her bills. Prior to her employment with the ambulance department, she had worked in hospitals as a surgical technician, then later as a phlebotomist. Eventually she became a nurse, as her mom had done before her. No doubt, she was a great nurse.

She was also the aggressor in most of her relationships. She told me she had been beaten up once by a man, and she vowed to never let another man hit her.

Clearly my female role model was not a "roll over and put up with it" type of woman. I saw my mom as a tough, take-charge person. She was not about to accept abuse from anyone. Not that she was hard-core. Far from it. Nothing seemed to phase her. That was her style of parenting as well. She didn't hover over me. She did, however, enroll me in dance classes rather than gymnastics since she feared I might break a bone on the mat or balance beam. I loved dancing. Since I had a tall, slender physique, I was pretty good at it, so I felt confident in junior high.

That confidence took a hit in high school. I tried out for the cheerleading squad twice and was rejected both times. I was devastated. My stepdad brought flowers to me, "just for trying," but my dreams were dashed. Worse yet, my best friend made the cheerleading squad when I hadn't.

Most of the friends I hung out with as a young teen in middle school were rebellious. They all smoked cigarettes, and I wanted to be like them—so when someone offered me a cigarette, I took it and inhaled a long drag. My eyes instantly watered, my throat burned, and I nearly choked to death! That was enough for me. And I've never had a desire to smoke tobacco since.

My friends knew every curse word ever invented and spewed profanity like unplugged fire hydrants. Naturally, I picked up some of the foul language as well. But when I walked up to my friends at the bus stop and threw out a cuss word trying to be cool, they seemed shocked. "Don't do that," one of my friends said, shaking her head from side to side.

So I didn't. I didn't drink or do drugs either, even though it would have been easy to access alcohol or illicit substances. Maybe I realized the potential problems those things presented, or maybe it was my nana's prayers—but for some reason, the drug and alcohol scene never attracted me even though I lived close to it.

With the swirl of evil all around me, it's a wonder I didn't turn out to be some sort of wild child. I did not attend church at that time. Yet surprisingly, I didn't spiral downward.

Dad lived on the outskirts of Tampa and was employed as an over-the-road truck driver, but we spent each weekend with Dad at his home, where he focused his attention on us for a few days before bringing us back to Mom.

Life at my dad's house was not perfect, but it was consistent. And that truly mattered. After four other marriages, when he and my stepmom, Wanda, found each other, they remained married for nearly forty years. We had home-cooked meals, and I felt safe and secure there. Once Dad asked me, "Jo Jo, what would you think about living with Dad for a while?"

"But what would I do on the weekends?" I asked innocently.

My mom's mom, Joanne Carol, whom I affectionately referred to as Nana, was also a role model to me, as were my aunts Carole, Leslie, and Susie. They were beautiful women, and I looked up to them. I admired their independent attitudes and wanted to be like them.

I was especially close with Nana, but while I was still a young girl, she went through a divorce and moved to Central Florida. Her new home, Avon Park, was a picturesque little town of less than ten thousand residents, surrounded by hundreds of thousands of acres of citrus trees. I didn't see Nana as frequently after she moved, and I missed her terribly.

Nana, who was light-skinned and had beautiful bluish-green eyes, looked nothing like my mom. With her dark eyes and dark skin, Mom was gorgeous; she resembled Poppa, my Native American grandfather, whose mother was a Cherokee.

I was built a lot like my nana, tall and slim, and we had similar personalities. I loved being with her, talking with her, and learning from her. She dressed in simple but stylish clothing and took good care of herself. She was a beautiful woman, and I admired her immensely. Nana was also a nurse who worked at our local hospital, so naturally, I wanted to become a nurse too. She looked so pretty in her white uniform and her nurse's cap.

In high school, I prepared for my future career by working as a certified nursing assistant, a designation I earned through my health classes. I planned to enroll in nursing school after my high school graduation. I wanted to be just like Nana and Mom.

Nana was also a godly, churchgoing woman. She knew my mom didn't often take me to church, so Nana always made sure we attended her church in Avon Park when I visited. She was serious about her faith, but not stuffy. Even though she dressed conservatively, especially when we went to church, she was not legalistic about such matters. She enjoyed dressing well. Away from church activities, unlike many women in ultraconservative Christian circles at that time, Nana was not opposed to throwing on a bathing suit and going swimming with me. And she looked good!

Although I didn't understand how such matters worked, I knew Nana prayed for me regularly, asking God to protect me, guide me, and draw me to Him. One of her big-time prayers was about to be answered, and I was totally unaware of it.

CHAPTER 3

Mr. Right

Mom remarried when I was fourteen, and life with her new husband, Fred, helped us feel like a "normal" family. Shortly after they married, they began attending a Pentecostal church together, so I went along with them one Sunday morning. I enjoyed the lively music and the interesting sermon, but neither of those affected me greatly. But there was a special presence in the service that I had never experienced previously. It was something different. It was God, and I knew it. I wanted to know Him.

As I stood singing with the congregation, a sense of warmth wrapped around me. It was as though love was washing over me, and I felt comforted and secure. I cried quietly, but not tears of sorrow or pain; they were tears of release and happiness. I didn't want the love and peace I experienced that day to ever go away.

That night, while alone in my bedroom, I said to myself and to God, "I don't know what is going on, but I want to continue feeling this way." He seemed to be seated right beside me, listening intently to the words pouring out of my heart. I knew something had changed in me; I could sense it, feel it, and I was changed for the better.

Some people say they found Jesus. Not me. Jesus found me, right there in my apartment bedroom. I was not in any sort of spiritual environment, yet He found me!

I was certain something had changed the first time I tried to watch a horror movie following that prayer in my bedroom. Prior to this day, I had been a big fan of horror movies, even the most occult sort of films. My aunts and I watched those movies and loved being scared half to death. But after those experiences in church and in my bedroom, I had no desire to see that stuff anymore. I thought, *God does not want me to watch this.*

I didn't know how to describe what had happened to me, or how to label it, so I wrote a letter to Nana. I told her what I had experienced in the church service and how differently I had felt after praying that night in my room. She wrote back to me within a few days and said, "Sandee Jo, I am so happy that I'm crying! You got saved!"

Saved? I had never heard that term in a spiritual context. Saved from what? It would take a while for me to understand that I had been saved from hell and given eternal life in the kingdom of God.

I wasn't familiar with church language and the expressions many Christians take for granted. All I knew was that my heart was full of joy. I felt clean and free, and I never wanted that to change.

I had no Christian friends. Other than Nana, the only other Christian I knew was my Great Aunt Pat, Nana's older sister, who still lived in the Tampa area. My mom and Fred didn't attend church regularly due to their job schedules, so Aunt Pat would often pick me up and take me along with her to a Baptist church.

Of course, any time I visited Nana in Avon Park, I attended services with her at the nondenominational Community Bible Church. One night when I was with her, she introduced me to the pastor's son, Tommy Schankweiler—a handsome, blue-eyed, blue-jean-clad believer with a bit of swagger. About five feet, ten inches tall, his body was slender and toned from hard work. "I'm so glad to meet you," he said, his eyes sparkling. "Your nana has spoken so highly of you."

I was hooked the moment I looked into those beautiful, deep blue eyes—much like those of my father—saw that quick, confident smile, and heard the subtle bravado in his voice. I liked him right away—almost surprising myself that I felt so delighted he had noticed me. Admittedly, my guard was down since Nana knew him and his family, but I'd be lying if I said I wasn't attracted to him. I was a new Christian, and I was impressed with this fine, God-honoring young man with his rugged cowboy type of good looks. I was a "city girl," so I thought he was different from most other fellows I'd met—a cut above, unique in many ways—and he captured my attention.

Since Tommy lived in Avon Park and I lived in Tampa, separated by a ninety-minute drive, we exchanged mailing addresses. For the next few months, we wrote letters to one another.

When I visited Nana, Tommy and I met at church and played board games at Nana's house. We continued our long-distance friendship, writing letters back and forth.

"Well, maybe Tommy could drive to Tampa to pick you up, and then drive you over here," Nana suggested. I knew I wouldn't feel comfortable riding an hour and a half with Tommy by myself. I'd be so nervous. I couldn't imagine talking with him for that long.

"Oh, Nana, I wouldn't even know what to say," I responded. But I continued to watch for his letters.

A few months into our pen pal relationship, Tommy sent a letter filling me in on his activities and proposing a possible date. He signed the letter, "Love, Tommy."

I wasn't used to that. I'd had a "puppy love" relationship with a friend in grade school, but that was the extent of my interaction with the opposite sex. I was fifteen years old, close to turning sixteen, and had never previously dated anybody, not even in a group—so I was nervous about going out alone with Tommy. As I entered my high school years, I stayed focused on my goal of becoming a nurse one day, so I didn't get distracted by dating. A senior football player in one of my classes took more than a casual interest in me, and though the other girls in my class were fawning over him and welcoming the attention of a popular upperclassman, I repeatedly rejected his advances. To me, he was simply annoying.

But Tommy was different. He was a young Christian man. And the more we wrote to one another, the more I liked him…a lot.

Nevertheless, I still felt uneasy when Tommy picked me up in his pickup truck. I sat as close to the door as possible and responded poorly to his feeble attempts at conversation.

For our first date, Tommy took me out for dinner at Spaghetti Warehouse, a casual Italian restaurant in Tampa that was part of a national chain. I dressed really cute, wearing a short—but not *too* short—dress and flat shoes, as I didn't want to appear taller than Tommy. Throughout the evening, he was a perfect gentleman. I liked him and appreciated his kindness, but I felt awkward the entire time. I was so nervous I could barely eat, and I felt bad about wasting Tommy's hard-earned money. During our conversation, I could never be sure if I was saying the right things or responding to Tommy's statements in a way that resonated with him.

Tommy told me he had been homeschooled most of his life, but he was hoping to attend a private Christian school for his last two years of high school.

"So what do you hope to do in life?" he asked. "What do you want to be?"

"I want to be become a nurse," I replied, "but I haven't figured it all out yet," I said honestly. "If I don't become a nurse, I want to be a stewardess, a flight attendant, and travel all over the world."

Tommy looked down at his plate and fiddled with his food. He later told me that when I expressed a desire to be a flight attendant, he didn't know what to think. *Well, she doesn't want to get married and have a family,* he wrongly assumed. According to Tommy's way of thinking at the time, a woman didn't carve out her own career unless it was something noble such as nursing or serving as a missionary.

Later I talked with my nana about my dinner with Tommy and said, "If that's what it feels like, I'm not ready for dating yet."

I sent Tommy a letter, saying, "I hope you don't hate me. You are a great person but I'm not ready to date yet."

Six months went by.

Nana called and said, "Tommy's birthday is coming up. Why don't you call him and wish him happy birthday?"

I thought that was a good idea.

Tommy's birthday was April 1, so I called him—and that's when we restarted our dating. Although we did some things I wanted to do, most of our dating activities centered around things he enjoyed, such as deer hunting and fishing. I had never hunted before and had only fished a few times, but I was intrigued with life in nature and didn't mind accompanying Tommy. And of course, we went to church. Tommy never asked me, "What would you like to do?" Really, he never went out of his way to do anything I wanted to do, which should have been a red flag to me. But I was young and in love and didn't recognize the selfishness Tommy displayed.

Tommy seemed to enjoy giving me instructions about what to do and what not to do in the woods and on the water. He was a perfectionist and wanted me to be the same. One of his sayings when hunting was, "When you shoot, you should only need one bullet. You get 'em the first time." Later he would teach that same adage to our sons.

Occasionally Tommy went hunting with his father for deer, elk, and bear in Pennsylvania and Northern Canada. They even went near the Arctic Circle hunting caribou, and he often brought down game in only one shot.

He obviously knew how to handle a gun well, and he had good aim.

CHAPTER 4

Dating the Prince

Dating the preacher's son had its advantages. Everywhere we went, people knew Tommy and greeted him respectfully. I was proud to be seen with him. Everyone assumed Tommy was a good guy, and he was—as far as anyone knew. He was kind to me, although he held rigid beliefs about the clothing I ought to wear and whether I should wear makeup. Women in his dad's congregation were meant to blend in, not stand out, he told me—and with my attractive, soon-to-be-seventeen-year-old features, long dark hair, and stylish clothes, I did not fit that image. When I wore a shorter than knee-length skirt with a cute blouse, I ruffled more than a few feathers, including Tommy's.

Tommy had three sisters who dressed like their mom, wearing only long skirts and high-collared dresses, revealing little skin. They wore hardly any makeup and never wore jewelry of any kind. We got along fine and found things in common to talk about, but no doubt, when they saw me wearing fashionable clothes, they may have worried about my morals.

Tommy's parents had already picked out a fine "holiness" young woman they hoped would pique their son's interest. She fit their favorite profile: no makeup, hair piled high on her head, and dressed in long dresses or skirts.

So when I first went to their home, they didn't exactly greet me with open arms. They were kind to me, but not warm and fuzzy by any means. The first time Tommy and his parents came to my house to have dinner with my parents, I dressed as I normally would have for a celebratory party. I picked out a cute white crop top, which revealed a few inches of bare midriff and fell off one of my bare shoulders. Then I thought, *They really like skirts,* so I picked out a short blue skirt. *This is going to be perfect!* To complete the outfit, I put on a pair of low heels.

It's a wonder Tommy's parents didn't try to cast the demons out of me! Nevertheless, they were sweet to me. Years later Tommy told me, "My parents accept you, but you were not the woman they wanted me to marry."

I couldn't imagine such a thing since I'd always felt likable.

When Tommy told me I'd have to change my look if we were to wed, I retorted, "You met and fell in love with me wearing these clothes. I'm not going to change just to marry you." We broke up over the phone, but despite the cautionary warnings of a close friend, I called Tommy and apologized after a few weeks. "I want to be together," I told him. And just like that, we were back on as a couple.

Slowly but surely, I submerged my wishes to his desires. For instance, prior to Tommy's influence, I was a confident young woman who expressed my personality through the way I dressed. I enjoyed dancing, and I modeled at an upscale clothing store at the local mall. When Tommy found out that guys were taking dance lessons in the same classes as me, he demanded that I quit. "I don't want any other guys dancing with you," he said. At the time, I considered his jealousy and possessiveness to be endearing qualities, thinking, *Oh, he adores me!* I was impressed that he wanted me all to himself, so I dropped out of my dance classes. Those same controlling traits of Tommy's would soon come to terrorize me.

We didn't have a lot of time for dating since we both held down part-time jobs during high school. I worked as a nursing assistant, and Tommy worked for his dad, helping to build houses around the church. He also earned some extra money doing roofing jobs in the area. Looking for something that offered healthcare benefits, Tommy took a job as a corrections officer, basically a prison guard, despite his father's opposition. "This will be good," Tommy told me. "After we get married, we'll have insurance."

Whoa, marriage! I was still getting comfortable with dating! Due to the distance between our homes, most of our dates occurred on Saturday or Sunday, when we had time to travel. Many of our dates revolved around church activities. I appreciated Tommy's dedication to the Lord and to serving in the church. He not only attended services on Sunday mornings and evenings, but on Wednesday evenings as well. So I was happy to go along with him when I was in Avon Park. And, of course, Nana was delighted to see us in church together.

I was mesmerized by the calm but authoritative fire-and-brimstone preaching of Tommy's father, Pastor Thomas Schankweiler Sr. He rarely raised his voice or flailed his arms in flamboyant gestures, yet the pastor presented strong countercultural messages that stirred my heart and challenged my mind. I liked the changes God was making in me, and I did not want to go back to my previously sinful lifestyle. I wanted to obey the Bible. I also saw and heard of the Schankweilers' genuine concern for people who were hurting. A pilot who owned his own plane, Pastor Schankweiler frequently flew humanitarian aid as well as spiritual materials to people in Haiti. Tommy accompanied him on several missions. Unlike Pastor Schankweiler—who was kind, loving, and benevolent—his son somehow developed a theologically incorrect attitude of overbearing patriarchy. He was forever telling me how to dress, how to speak, and with whom I could hang out. His view was that the husband is the boss, and the wife's place is subservient to his. It wasn't "My way or the highway"; it was "My way is the *only* way."

For his last two years of high school, Tommy transferred to Hobe Sound, a private Christian boarding school on the other side of the state, about two hours away from his home and about three hours from mine. "Since I've been homeschooled all my life," he told me, "I'd like to experience what it's like to have classmates." During this time Tommy drove across Florida to visit with me. We continued our long-distance dating relationship for a year and a half.

CHAPTER 5

Kidnapped at the Wedding

*T*ommy and I started dating regularly when I was only sixteen years of age; we got engaged when I was seventeen years old. Although I still saw nursing school in my future, Tommy and I were married on October 21, 1989, just five days after my eighteenth birthday. Pastor Thomas Schankweiler Sr. and Tommy's Uncle Fred conducted a simple, traditional ceremony at Forest Hills Church of the Nazarene, my great-grandmother's church in Tampa. My mom planned most of the wedding details, but Tommy wanted one of the groomsmen, James Crocker, to play Bette Midler's hit song "The Rose" on his saxophone during the ceremony. That was fine with me. Oddly, the guys in our wedding party were mostly complete strangers to me. I knew only Tommy and my brother, Billy. Except for Tommy's parents, whom I already knew, I met the remainder of the wedding party at the rehearsal dinner.

My attendants included Tommy's sister, my cousin, two of my close friends, and my stepsister. My great-grandmother, a florist, provided and arranged all the wedding flowers.

The church was packed with people, many of whom had driven across Florida to attend the wedding along with my Tampa family.

It was easy to tell which guests had been invited by my family and me, and which had been invited by Tommy and his family—especially the women. Nearly all of my female guests were decked out in party clothes and flowing hairstyles, while most of Tommy's female guests wore plain dresses and their hair in tight buns atop their heads.

I felt like a princess, radiantly happy as I walked down the aisle. I couldn't suppress a smile when Nana called out, "You look beautiful, Sis!" as I passed by. I stopped, lifted my veil, and kissed my mom who was sitting in the front row.

After the wedding ceremony, the guests and bridal party gathered in the church fellowship hall for refreshments of homemade punch and finger foods provided by people from the church. We had a wedding cake with royal blue icing. We did not have a meal; nor was there any alcohol or dancing at our wedding. Tommy and I cut our cake and opened wedding gifts, and I tossed the bridal bouquet. Then we simply enjoyed being with our family and friends.

Near the close of the celebration, as an entertaining "down home" way of generating a special wedding gift for the newlyweds, several groomsmen swept me away from the reception, ostensibly "kidnapped" me, until my groom could raise enough money from the wedding attendees to "ransom" his bride. It was a fun way to get some honeymoon cash. While Tommy worked the reception crowd, begging for their financial assistance, I was blindfolded and hustled into a pickup truck along with two groomsmen I had only met the previous night at the rehearsal dinner. My captors drove off into the night, giving the groom time to evoke sympathy and cash from the bemused wedding guests. One of those kidnapping groomsmen, James Crocker, had attended the eleventh grade at Hobe Sound Bible School with Tommy in 1987 and knew more about my groom than he let on. James knew Tommy as "Cowboy"—a funny, smart, "countrified" fellow—and considered him a best friend at school. He had also witnessed Tommy's rebellious, duplicitous side, which I had never seen. James knew Tommy chewed tobacco—definitely a no-no in the Schankweiler family—and stashed a pornographic magazine under his mattress in the dormitory. He and Tommy were buddies and had kept in touch prior to our wedding.

All I knew about James at the time was that he was a gregarious groomsman who assisted in the "kidnapping." But as Tommy and I drove off in his truck, which my maid of honor had decorated with balloons, toilet paper, and shaving cream, I was soon to discover the evil that James knew about and much more.

CHAPTER 6

The Honeymoon Is Over

*F*ollowing our wedding, Tommy and I enjoyed a weeklong honeymoon in Maggie Valley, North Carolina. Everything seemed ideal, and I was so happy simply to be together. We had never previously spent prolonged periods of time together due to the distance between our homes. Now, at last, we had plenty of time to enjoy one another. Everything was perfect. The mountain air was cool and crisp, the leaves were turning bright colors, and the fall foliage looked as though God had personally painted the forest just for us, using every color in His palette.

We enjoyed a week in the mountains and then headed back to Avon Park. Compared to Tampa, Avon Park was a quiet, sleepy town where folks were friendly and "helpful," meaning everyone knew everyone else's business. But I welcomed the closeness of the community. I looked forward to setting up a house and was excited to be Tommy's wife. We arrived at our new address—a simple but brand-new double-wide trailer—tired and exhausted from the travel but happy to be home.

Tommy and I went to work unloading our belongings from his pickup truck. Carrying two bags full of dirty clothes, I stepped inside our trailer and stopped to take in the moment. I stood in the middle of the living room, basking in the joy of being married, and gazing all around at every detail of our new home. Although I had seen the double-wide during previous trips to Avon Park and in the prewedding moving process, I hadn't really spent much time in the trailer. Tommy's dad had helped him get it ready for us, and Nana had helped me do a bit of decorating. Now, as I looked around, it felt like home. *Perfect*, I thought with a smile.

I was still daydreaming of all the good things that would happen in our new home when Tommy came through the front door and began verbally attacking me and berating me for taking too long. He roughly pushed me, shoving me to the floor, yelling at me the whole time. Looking up at Tommy, I was shocked and horrified, afraid to move. I had never before seen this aggressive side of his personality. There had been no previous warning signs. Quite the opposite, he had always been so kind to me, treating me like a princess. I was stunned.

I picked myself up off the floor and continued about the business of unpacking. But my heart and mind were deeply troubled and confused. What was this? How could Tommy suddenly switch from Mr. Nice Guy to a such an overbearing monster?

Later, Tommy apologized. "I'm so sorry," he said. "I promise it will never happen again. Please forgive me."

I nodded slowly, and said, "I understand," even though I didn't. "I forgive you."

That's all Tommy needed to hear, and we went on as though nothing odd had happened.

Tommy and I continued setting up housekeeping in the rural area of Avon Park, Florida. There were no beaches close by, and we didn't have a shopping mall, which felt like a cultural shock for me. But we had lots of churches. Our church was located on County Road 17A.

We lived in the same vicinity as Tommy's mom and dad, in a sort of spiritual compound in which many of the homes were built by Tommy's family. Tommy's friends were mostly guys he worked with, and we had only a few couples friends beyond those who attended Pastor Schankweiler's church. Most of the people living in the community attended the church at the front of the enclave, so it was a natural decision for us to attend the church his dad pastored. It was the spiritual community in which Tommy had grown up, and of course, everyone knew him there as the pastor's son. We went to church every Sunday morning and Sunday evening. We attended Wednesday evening prayer service, camp meetings, and any other special services. If the church was open, we were there. Our lives revolved around the church. Later Tommy became the youth leader, and we both served in the bus ministry, which drove around to pick up children and bring them to Sunday school each week. The service style was traditional "holiness," which meant the congregation was enthusiastic but rather staid. Our music was mostly piano and organ—Tommy's mom alternated playing both—and we sang the old hymns of the church. I loved music and had rarely heard the hymns previously, so I enjoyed the melodies and learned a lot from the lyrics.

The pastor, Tommy's dad, was a good, godly man who was not afraid to speak out against evil and had no qualms about calling out sin. I appreciated the messages, especially because I was such a new believer and theologically uneducated. I soaked up Pap's teachings about the Bible.

Tommy attended with me and never let on that he was anything but a model Christian, so I assumed his outburst following our honeymoon was merely the result of stress and an emotional aberration.

I couldn't have been more wrong.

Tommy was a control freak who wanted to run everything about our marriage, especially me. He repeatedly told me what clothes I could and should not wear. I loved the lessons of style I had learned from my mom and my three aunts, all of whom dressed fashionably and had taught me to do the same. They had also taught me how to do my makeup and hair. For my birthday one year, my Aunt Carole had bought me a beautiful canary yellow dress with big buttons, big sleeves, and squared shoulder pads. I loved that dress! It was so pretty and made me feel beautiful and so feminine when I wore it.

I had worn the yellow dress on a few dates with Tommy when we were first getting to know each other. I'd even worn it to my bridal shower. He seemed to like it, too, and had commented on how nice I looked in it.

But once we were married, Tommy's opinion of that dress—and me in it—changed drastically. I put it on one morning to wear to church, but before we walked out the door together, Tommy scowled at me. "Go change into something else," he said gruffly. "Why do you want to wear flashy clothes like that? To attract men?"

"No, Tommy," I said. "That's silly."

"I never want to see you in that dress again."

"Tommy, there is nothing wrong with this dress. Look, the length comes all the way to my knee, and the neckline is not revealing. What's wrong with wearing this to church?"

"It's too brightly colored," he responded.

At first I thought he was joking.

He wasn't.

"You shouldn't stand out when you walk into a room. You should blend in."

It wasn't worth an argument before church services, so I went and changed my dress. But more and more, I felt my own personality slipping away and being replaced by a woman shaped in Tommy's warped image of what a woman should be.

Tommy often accused me of dressing provocatively because I wore jeans and short-sleeved blouses rather than long frumpy dresses. He demanded that I "cover" myself and wear clothes that de-emphasized my figure and my femininity.

Even while driving, if Tommy saw a guy pull up in a car next to us and glance in my direction, he thought the guy was trying to seduce me. "Quit looking at that guy!" he'd yell. Usually I hadn't even noticed the man, but Tommy seemed convinced that other men were trying to steal me away from him—and he wasn't going to allow that to happen. His jealousy was both endearing and frightening—endearing because Tommy felt possessive of me, but frightening because he often said, "If I can't have you, nobody else will."

A couple of times, Tommy got out of his truck at a red light to confront the man in the next lane because he'd looked at me.

Not only did he want to control what I wore, but also where I could go and with whom, what to cook and how. He gave specific orders regarding how he wanted the laundry done and how he wanted the seams of his prison guard uniform ironed. Tommy had grown up with a stay-at-home mom, and Sally Schankweiler was meticulous about taking care of her home and family. I had grown up with a mom who worked outside the home, so prior to our marriage, I hadn't learned a lot of basic housekeeping skills. "You need to go see my mom," Tommy said, "and she will teach you how to make mashed potatoes." (I honestly thought mashed potatoes came from a box!) Whenever my homemaking abilities didn't meet Tommy's expectations, or didn't match the level of his mother's skill, he exploded with fury—sometimes violently.

He always apologized after an outburst, and because we enjoyed many good times in between our arguments, it was easy for me to dismiss his cruel words and make excuses for his erratic and controlling behavior. I was young and to me, an apology made everything okay.

It didn't.

I wasn't proud of our behavior; honestly, I was embarrassed by it, so maybe that is why I didn't mention our troubles to anyone else. Besides, early on, I retaliated when Tommy did something to hurt me. Whatever he did to me, I did right back to him. I kicked, punched, spit—whatever it took to defend myself. I knew I couldn't overpower him, but that didn't keep me from trying.

On one occasion, our fight resulted in the spaghetti I had cooked for dinner being splattered all over the walls, ceiling, and floor of our trailer. Smashed plates and overturned pots littered the floor. Tommy got so angry he whipped a barbed broadhead hunting arrow right at my face, but I moved and he missed. The arrow grazed the top of my shoulder, and I yelped in pain. But without a moment's hesitation, I snatched a huge knife out of the butcher block we had just gotten as a wedding gift. I threw the knife at him as hard as I could. Fortunately, my aim was no better than Tommy's, and I missed as well.

Later that day, when things had calmed down a bit, I called Nana. "Please come pick me up," I said. "I'm not staying here." I didn't use the word *rescue*, but she got my drift. She didn't ask for reasons, and in a matter of minutes, she and my step-grandpa pulled up in the driveway. Tommy met them at the front door.

"We've come to get Sandee Jo," Nana said quietly but firmly.

Tommy must have sensed that Nana suspected something was wrong because he retorted brusquely, "She isn't going with you. She's not going anywhere."

"Well, she called her nana and asked us to pick her up," my step-grandfather said.

"She's my wife, and she's not going anywhere with you," Tommy said coldly. He closed the door in my grandparents' faces.

They didn't argue, but Nana and her husband had looked past Tommy and seen the inside of our brand-new trailer—the walls spattered with spaghetti sauce and the broken dishes littering the kitchen floor. They went immediately to Pastor Tom and his wife, Sally, and told them something was awry.

Although I didn't hear the phone, Tommy's dad must have called—because the next thing I knew, Tommy had grasped my hand tightly and said, "Come on. We're going down to my dad's house and we're going to talk."

"I don't want to go to your dad's house to talk," I said.

"Come on!" Tommy said loudly, pulling me toward the door. We walked down the street to his parents' house. Tommy's firm grip never loosened as we walked.

My grandparents were still talking with the Schankweilers when Tommy and I arrived at the pastor's home. Although I heard none of their conversation, the expressions on their faces were solemn. Then my grandparents went outside to their car as Tommy and I stepped inside the Schankweiler home.

I was unprepared for my mother-in-law's acerbic greeting. "I hope you're happy," she said to me with a hint of a snarl. "Look at what you've caused." Her accusatory tone took me aback and made me nervous. I loved Sally and still do to this day. She was a tough woman, but she was also willing to help. Perhaps she thought I was dragging baggage from my upbringing into my relationship with her son. *Maybe what happened was my fault after all*, I thought. In the early days of our marriage, I never backed down from Tommy, not even when he turned violent. But Sally's jumping to conclusions made me feel unfairly blamed. I wanted to bolt out the door, climb into my grandparents' car, and ride off with them.

But I felt that running away wasn't the answer, so I went out and told my grandparents that I was going to stay. "I don't want to lose my marriage," I told them. I went back inside to talk with Tommy's parents. We sat down with them in the living room and proceeded to have an informal marriage counseling session. Tommy's parents did most of the talking.

It wasn't much of a session, and it was even less counseling. Tommy and I sat on his parents' couch, and Tommy said, "We had an argument." I remained quiet and didn't tell Tommy's parents about his violent outbursts toward me. But I think they knew. Nevertheless, to this day, I'm not sure they realized how severe Tommy's abusive behavior could be. Neither Tommy's mom nor dad saw the mess in our house. I felt judged, as though everything that had transpired that day had been my fault, and even though I believed that wasn't the truth, I was a people-pleaser who wanted everyone to be happy.

Pastor Schankweiler spoke with a calm but authoritative voice. "A husband and wife have to be a team," he said. He delivered his words carefully and without blame, but that may have been a counterproductive approach. Tommy might have responded to a firm rebuke from his father, but none came. Instead, we both agreed we had let things get out of hand and needed to take steps to change our behavior.

Still, their questions put the onus on me rather than Tommy. Didn't I want to break the cycle of divorce in our family? Didn't I dream of a marriage that lasts, that wouldn't break up in divorce?

I mumbled vague responses to their questions indicating that yes, I wanted our marriage to work.

"Well, if that's so, then staying together and working through these problems is the right thing to do," Tommy's parents agreed. They arranged for us to see a counselor—not simply Tommy and me, but all four of us together. We later went to one session. One. That was the only session we ever attended.

I couldn't tell if Tommy's parents were reading between the lines or not, but after an hour or so, we left—just as estranged as we were before we visited with the pastor and his wife.

Maybe worse because we had sought help and failed to find it.

It wasn't long before I put away the stylish clothes I had worn most of my life. I adapted my wardrobe to include light sweaters and dresses to cover my body so the bruises Tommy inflicted on my arms, chest, and shoulders could not be seen. Worse yet were the unseen, hidden wounds to my heart, mind, and spirit.

CHAPTER 7

Mind Control

*I*n the aftermath of the incident witnessed by Nana and my step-grandfather, Tommy refused to allow me to go places with Nana any longer. Nor would he permit her to step inside our home. That was hard for me. I didn't want Tommy to drive a wedge between my family and me, but I felt that, after God, my top priority now was my relationship with my husband. So once again, and against my better judgment, I acquiesced.

The relationship between Nana and the Schankweilers was never the same. Shortly after the incident, Nana and her husband left Pastor Schankweiler's church to worship with another fellowship across town. Nana had her reasons, she said, but I felt deep inside that the true explanation involved the awkwardness she felt. After all, she had alerted Pastor Schankweiler of a potential problem, but he had failed to provide the help her granddaughter needed. Over time the interfamily relationships improved...but not much.

In the early months of our marriage, Tommy and I enjoyed many good times together. We didn't have much money, but with the little we had, Tommy made upgrades to our home's exterior and landscaping. I worked inside, decorating and hanging pictures. I also worked harder at learning to cook. I experimented with recipes I thought Tommy might enjoy. The one meal I felt confident about was chicken and yellow rice. I could make that with my eyes closed because I had grown up on that meal. I was also pretty good at fixing a pot of spaghetti in a hurry.

The television cooking channels didn't exist in those days, so I didn't have the luxury of learning from them—and it wouldn't have mattered if they had been on the air anyway. We owned a television with rabbit ears—no cable TV for us—so we received only a few stations, and even they were fuzzy. Due to Tommy's strict religious rules, television was discouraged. We would occasionally rent a movie—always a general audience fare—but that was our only video connection to the outside world. Still, we had fun and life seemed good.

Our mobile home sat on a corner lot, at the base of a hill leading to a thick orange grove. The trees provided shade and privacy—sometimes too much privacy. The home next to us was owned by some folks from up north, who used it as an escape from the cold northern winters. These snowbird neighbors were seldom seen for months at a time.

Tommy continued working as a corrections officer during the evening shift from four o'clock in the afternoon until midnight. On his days off, he laid fresh sod in our yard and installed a sprinkler system to keep it well watered in the Florida heat. He also added some pretty stonework to the base of our double-wide trailer, giving it a polished look. Later he added a shed onto the side of our house and put an awning over a carport. At my request, he put up a clothesline so I could dry our clothes outdoors in the fresh air. Tommy built a concrete pen for his hunting dogs, complete with plumbing and a chain-link fence surrounding it so they could move freely without leashes. The dog pen looked like a resort for canines!

Tommy was good with his hands and was incredibly creative. I was convinced there was nothing he could not do if he put his mind to it. If one of our vehicles stopped running, Tommy fixed it. If something broke inside the house, Tommy repaired it. He mowed our lawn, planted trees and shrubs, and made our double-wide look like an upscale home in the community.

To help with our expenses, I babysat a couple of toddlers for a family in town. I kept the children in our home during the day, but the toddlers often made noise while Tommy was trying to sleep.

Consequently, I took a job at a local faith-based daycare center. I enjoyed working with the children there, and Tommy could sleep undisturbed at home before going to work. My responsibilities included caring for the class of three-year-olds each day and teaching them God's Word from curriculum, books, videos, and music. The kids were like little sponges, soaking up the Scripture, memorizing verses, and learning the stories. And so was I!

As a relatively new believer myself who had never attended Sunday school or any other Bible classes, I was thrilled. I was learning right along with the children! The simple songs played over and over in my head long after I clocked out from work, and the Bible verses I helped the kids memorize became embedded in my mind and heart as well.

But all too soon the violence in our home erupted again, in many of the same forms. It almost felt like we were characters in the movie *Groundhog Day*, the actions and words being replayed again and again. The difference, of course, was that rather than repetition producing love as depicted in the movie, the violence destroyed it.

A few months into our marriage, my dad and stepmom called to invite us to a Saturday get-together at their home near Lakeland, Florida. Tommy had planned a hunting trip with his friends, so he did not want to go—and, growing increasingly more paranoid about any time I spent away from home, he made it quite clear that he didn't want me to go either. "I don't like you leaving town without me," he said.

Tommy left with his buddies, and I pouted. After a while I thought, *I don't want to sit home by myself all day on a Saturday.* I jotted a note on a piece of paper, informing Tommy that I was going to Lakeland for the day and would see him later. We had no cell phones at the time, so there was no way I could have reached him in the woods to inform him of my plans.

I drove to Lakeland by myself and enjoyed the afternoon simply hanging out with my family members and catching up. At one point my stepsister and I went for a ride, and when we returned to our parents' house, my stepbrother Calvin met me outside. "Tommy called while you were gone," he said. "And he sounded mad." I could tell Calvin was trying to be kind, to play the role of peacemaker, so I looked back at him inquisitively. "And?"

"Well…" My stepbrother hesitated. "He said, 'Tell my m-----f------ wife to get her a-- home!'" Although he didn't say so, my step-brother must have thought, *That's unusual language for a preach-er's son.*

"What?" I could not believe Tommy would be so rude and profane to one of my family members. Yes, he had spewed those kinds of obscenities to me in private, but he normally guarded his behavior and conversation around his family and mine.

I was hurt and embarrassed. I tried to cover Tommy's unac-ceptable behavior by saying, "Oh, he's just trying to be funny." But I knew better, and I was furious!

I left the family outing and drove the distance between Lakeland and Avon Park as fast as I dared. As soon as I pulled into our driveway, I jammed the truck into park, the tires screeching on the pavement. I jumped out, slammed the door behind me, and stomped into the house to confront him. "How could you do that to my family?" I said. I was so mad at him and wanted to give him a piece of my mind.

Tommy met me at the door and yelled back at me, just as mad. The confrontation escalated quickly, and Tommy grabbed me and threw me up against the wall. He began hitting me violently and yanking my hair.

I kicked my feet at him, fighting back in every way I knew how. When he lost his grip on me, I quickly slid away and bolted out the back door, running into the orange grove adjacent to our home, hoping to escape his blows. I ran as fast as I could, picking my way through the thick maze of trees and sandy soil, with Tommy chasing close behind me.

The soft soil made running difficult, as did the skirt I was wearing. I kicked off my open-toed slip-on shoes so I could run faster and continued running barefoot, the thicket scraping against my legs as I ran. I was scared and tears streamed down my face. Tommy spotted some old oranges on the ground and pounced on the opportunity. He pelted me with the hard oranges he picked up, hitting me in the back and head again and again. I tried to evade the vicious, stonelike blows to my body, but I was worn-out; my foot caught on the ground, and I tripped and fell forward into the sand, landing face-first. In a flash, Tommy tackled me and pinned me down. I screamed but knew it was futile to cry out. We were in the middle of an orange grove, far from anyone's ability to hear. "Get up!" Tommy roared. "You're gonna walk home, and you're not gonna run away. Get up and walk." Tommy grabbed at my body, yanked me to my feet by my hair, shouting curses at me all the while. He dragged me back to our double-wide, threw me inside, pulled the telephone out of the wall, and locked all the doors. He went outside and ripped the alternator wires off the truck engine, then returned to the house and continued glaring at me venomously, guarding me so I couldn't run again.

I stared back at him quietly, keeping my thoughts to myself. I was learning that what I wanted, what I thought and felt, really didn't matter much to Tommy. Not that I was a doormat by any means. When I disagreed with him, I told him so. I expressed my opinions and my own ideas vociferously. But I soon learned that my opinions, thoughts, or ideas had no place in our marriage according to him. He was determined, whether he was right or wrong, that I had but two choices. I could agree with him and life would go smoothly, or I could verbalize my ideas and suffer the consequences. Increasingly, I felt overpowered by his forceful opinions and, in time, stopped expressing myself to him unless I knew he agreed with me. To do otherwise invited trouble, and it wasn't worth the verbal and physical repercussions.

Why didn't I leave when I realized this abusive part of Tommy's personality was not merely an aberration but a serious problem?

I wish I knew.

Why didn't I reach out to someone for help?

Maybe I was too young and naïve. Or maybe I was hopeful that he would change back into the Tommy I knew when we first met— the kind of person I believed he was capable of being.

I also truly believed I loved him, so I told myself the things I wanted to hear: *No husband is perfect. He's a hard worker. Maybe I've caused his outbursts.*

Moreover, I knew most relationships had their ups and downs, so I didn't reach out to my family. I didn't want them to think poorly of Tommy, or to hate him for his mistreatment of me. And I certainly didn't want our marriage to end in divorce, as had so many others in my extended family.

Inevitably, after the heat of our arguments and our emotions calmed down, Tommy would apologize and tell me how much he loved me. His aggression seemed to vanish as quickly as it had appeared, and suddenly he'd become tender and super-attentive to my needs. Usually he'd want to have sexual relations after a fight, as though sexual union could somehow make up for the horrible things he had said and done. My brain, body, and heart weren't ready for physical intimacy. We had just had a major blowup, and Tommy wanted physical intercourse. His actions were confusing, awkward, and uncomfortable for me, but I complied even though sexual intimacy was the last thing on my mind after his outbursts. I didn't want him to touch me. But his guilt was obvious, and he seemed so sorry and contrite that I usually submitted to his desires. I was simply relieved the abuse was over, and hopeful it wouldn't happen again.

But it always did.

Although Tommy's physical threats were constant, the power and control his words had over my mind were equally as potent, if not more so—and he knew it. He expertly manipulated me, playing on my emotions one minute, then terrorizing me the next. Even if he wasn't verbalizing threats, his large calloused hands had a vocabulary of their own. After I had felt their strength around my neck or pulling my hair, I could never forget those awful feelings. I knew the power of his words, and I also knew the force of those hands. Together they played havoc with my mind.

An amateur but skillful taxidermist, Tommy and his dad had built a small shed behind our house where Tommy worked at his hobby. He'd thought about developing it into a business but didn't think it would be profitable enough to support us. He crafted some special pieces that he sold to a few customers, but mostly his shop was for his enjoyment.

Tommy reminded me that he possessed certain lethal chemicals in his shed. "I have all I need to completely disintegrate human bones," he told me one day as I interrupted his work. "Do you see that?" He pointed to a small dish on the workbench. "That used to be an animal's leg." I stared at the bowl filled with a hazy, grainy liquid. "I can make bones disappear," Tommy said. Although the macabre threat was not overt, the implications seemed obvious.

CHAPTER 8

Baby Blues

At first, it was easy to think, *If he hits me again, I'll just leave.* And even though Tommy was a strong guy, I fought back when we argued, defending myself. If he threw something at me, I threw something right back at him. Sometimes, he'd hit me hard with his hand, and on several occasions, I suffered black eyes—but I always hit him back.

But when I became pregnant, I stopped fighting back because I was afraid Tommy's blows would hurt the baby. We had been married about five months when we discovered I was expecting our first child. I was so excited! Tommy's initial reaction to the news was less than stellar. "It's too soon," he told me. "I'm not ready to be a father. We're too young." Looking back, he was probably right about that, but his lack of enthusiasm did not dull mine.

I called my mom to tell her the news, but she didn't answer the phone. I called again and still no one answered, so I left her a message. "Mom, please call me as soon as you get this!" I didn't tell her the reason for my call.

A while later, I was outside hanging clothes on the clothesline when I heard the telephone ringing inside the house. Assuming that Mom was returning my call, I hastily ran back around the house toward the front door—but the sand on the bottoms of my shoes sent me skidding across the carport pavement like I was on an ice-skating rink. I landed violently on the concrete, scraping my knees and palms. My bloody knees stung with pain from tiny rock fragments stuck in the skin, and my palms were red and raw. My entire body ached.

How careless of me! I scolded myself. I had just learned that I was carrying a five-week-old child within me, and I worried that my fall had done some damage. Thankfully, it had not, but that was another warning to me to avoid conflict with Tommy. I didn't want to risk losing our baby to one of his violent temper tantrums. Increasingly, my impulse was to protect the tiny life within me— even if that meant holding my tongue or letting Tommy have his way simply to keep the peace.

For most of the pregnancy, that plan worked fairly well. I avoided conflicts with Tommy as much as possible, caving on almost every occasion when even the hint of friction increased. But just a few days before our baby was due, Tommy and I got into another intense argument, and in a matter of moments, it turned physical. Tommy slapped me across the face with his strong palm, knocking me to the floor. I knew better than to fight back, especially with my big belly. Because I did not want to risk harm to our baby, I simply hunkered down and attempted to block or deflect Tommy's blows as best I could. One of his slaps caught the corner of my left eye, and I knew immediately it was going to swell. I continued lying on the floor, and without any resistance, he got bored and stormed away from me.

I lay there a few more moments to make sure he was gone, then got up and put ice on my eye—but it was too late. It was already red, and the skin all around my eye was turning an ugly bluish purple down the side of my face.

For the next few days, I covered the swollen welt with heavy makeup—much to Tommy's chagrin—but the discoloration all around my eye was still obvious when my water broke at five a.m. on December 29, 1990.

Tommy took me to the hospital, and although the nurses and doctor noticed my eye, they were more concerned that the baby was healthy, as was I.

Our first baby, a beautiful little boy, was born barely fourteen months after our wedding day. We named him Thomas James Schankweiler III to honor Tommy and Pastor Schankweiler. Since that was a mouthful for such a little tyke, we called him Bubba to differentiate between his dad's and grandfather's names.

The next morning, when the doctor examined me, he looked at the puffiness surrounding my eye and asked, "Did you break some capillaries while pushing?"

"I don't know," I answered semi-truthfully.

"Hmm," he said. "That sometimes happens." He expressed no further concern.

Although the medical staff did not make a big deal about my black eye, my family members noticed it immediately when they arrived to see the baby and me. "What happened?" they asked with genuine concern.

"Oh, I fell into the corner of the fireplace a couple nights ago," I lied. By then I had grown quite skilled at lying—something I had rarely ever done before meeting Tommy. But now I lied so often to cover for Tommy, I sometimes convinced myself I was telling the truth—which, of course, I was not.

Especially because Mom and Nana had nursing backgrounds, I had to choose my deceptions carefully. Nevertheless, they knew that sometimes pregnant women in late stages can easily lose their balance and fall, so they seemed to believe my story. Or, at least, their happiness in seeing the new life overshadowed any negative distractions.

Bubba had beautiful blue eyes, and when I held him in my arms, he felt perfect. I couldn't help hoping this child would change Tommy, that the joys of fatherhood would help him be the man we both wanted him to be. Once Bubba was born, Tommy was much happier, and he truly loved our son. He seemed proud to be a dad—but unfortunately, parenthood did not magically transform Tommy into a different person.

Our arguments continued even though we now had an infant in the house, and many turned into vicious fights after Bubba was born. Rather than bringing out the best in himself to become a good father, Tommy used our baby as leverage to get what he wanted and used our son to intensify my fear of him. He frequently said things such as, "If you ever separate me from my boy, I will do the unthinkable. Now, more than ever, you can never leave me. I simply won't allow that to happen." Then, to emphasize his threat, he said, "If you leave, I will drive to Tampa and kill your entire family."

Of course I worried he might kill our baby as well. Because I had so often been the victim of Tommy's rage, I believed his threats were credible and felt he was unstable enough to carry out the most horrific acts.

Despite the tension in our relationship, I got along remarkably well with Tommy's parents and family members. Pap was especially helpful. My father-in-law guided me spiritually, not merely through his preaching, but also through his example as a kind, compassionate man. His heart for the Lord and his commitment to missions—especially in impoverished Haiti—impressed me and made me want to grow stronger in my faith. I knew I could ask him anything about the Bible, and if he didn't know the answer, he would research the matter and follow up with me. He was never too proud to say, "I don't know. I need to study more to find out." Thanks to Pap, I felt I was learning and growing spiritually stronger.

But I never mentioned a word to him about his son's abusive behaviors.

My mother-in-law, Sally (Granny) Schankweiler, was a marvelous homemaker. She was talented in the kitchen and could whip up tasty meals in no time, making the preparation of a full course dinner look easy. She was also good at sewing, gardening, and even woodworking. She crafted numerous unique pieces of furniture and decorative items around their home and taught me how to make some cute clothing for Bubba too. We talked often, but I never broached the subject of Tommy's uncontrolled temper.

Many people from the Avon Park community attended their church, which was within walking distance of our house. I felt accepted by my new church family and regularly took part in the activities of the church. I worked in the nursery with the children and helped with Vacation Bible School during the summer. Later I'd work at the church-sponsored daycare center, as well as at an elementary school. I often helped in the kitchen when we had special meals or during camp meeting services at the church. Most of the women with whom I came in contact were part of the church, and I enjoyed being around them, learning from them, as they offered me their wisdom about life.

Of course Nana lived nearby too, just a few miles away, even though she no longer attended that same church. Nevertheless, I saw her often, and she taught me about housekeeping and how to manage a budget, how to find good deals at the grocery store, and other basic skills necessary for a young wife and mother.

I missed my mom and being able to see her anytime I wanted, but I accepted that as one of the adjustments of being married and living on my own with my husband. She came to Avon Park occasionally to visit Nana and me, and I was always glad to see her. But I never told her about Tommy's abusive behavior.

Shortly after Bubba was born, Tommy and I had another blowup. As usual, following the fight, Tommy was "repentant" and especially attentive to my needs. When the smoke cleared and I knew he was still feeling bad about the way he had treated me, I decided to take advantage of his "good-heartedness."

I asked him, "Would it be okay if I drove to Tampa so my mom can see the baby?"

Still "penitent," Tommy said, "Yes, that's fine." He rolled over and went to sleep.

I didn't waste a moment but hurriedly threw a bag together for Bubba and me before Tommy had time to change his mind.

In truth, I didn't want to merely visit my mom. I wanted time to think. I had contemplated leaving Tommy and needed some space to figure out how I might do that safely. Of course I couldn't tell Tommy that, or he'd have never allowed me to leave the house.

I took off for Tampa with baby Bubba. When I arrived at Mom's house, I felt relieved simply to be away from all the chaos in my own home. After a brief time of oohing and aahing over the baby, I told my mom and Fred, my stepdad, that Tommy and I had had an argument and that I needed some time to clear my head. They didn't seem greatly concerned. "Well, that's what young married couples do," they said. "Couples sometimes get into arguments."

I didn't tell them about the physical aspects of our arguments. I knew they liked Tommy, and I didn't want to ruin their relationship with him. Besides, I was still holding on to the hope that one day he would be a different man, and when that day came, I didn't want my family members to hate him for his previous abusive behavior.

I hadn't been in Tampa long before Tommy called. "It's time for you to come home," he said.

"I just got here," I told him. "I'm going to stay a little longer than I had planned."

Tommy's tone grew suspicious. He knew I was safely out of his reach, so he couldn't control me physically. So he used another tactic: He surprised me by weeping uncontrollably over the telephone. He had a sad Keith Whitley song playing in the background. He apologized for hurting me and begged me to give him one more chance. "My life would not be the same without you and the baby," he cried over the line.

The man knew how to manipulate my emotions. Tommy knew that more than anything in life, I wanted a whole and happy family. He played the family card with adept skill.

And I fell for it. We hung up, but not before my voice softened.

But Tommy wasn't content yet.

A few hours after I hung up the phone, Tommy pulled his truck into Mom and Fred's driveway. "I've come to follow you home," he announced. He had driven an hour and a half out of his way to make sure I returned home.

Fred suggested, "Why don't the two of you go for a little ride and talk?"

I looked at my mom and Fred and shrugged. They kept the baby as Tommy and I went out to his car. Before we left, Tommy insisted we have sex—so we did, right there in the car in the driveway. That was Tommy's way of making everything all right.

Afterward, we went for a short drive, and when we returned to the house, I packed Bubba's bag and mine and got in my car to head back to Avon Park, with Tommy following close behind me.

I was foolish to go back with him. I've often wondered how my life might have been different had I left Tommy for good that day.

Would he have retaliated if I had stayed at Mom's and filed for divorce? Would he have gone through with the divorce and then sought to make my life miserable by harassing me? Would he have fought to get our baby?

I'll never know the answers to those questions because I dutifully drove back to Avon Park instead. From that time on, Tommy cinched the noose tighter around me. He realized that he had almost lost control of me, and he was not about to allow that to happen again. My trips to Tampa became fewer and fewer because he feared I might leave him. The only time he permitted me to travel was when I went with Nana and returned with her, usually within the same day. He disguised his controlling spirit by saying, "I worry about you traveling alone with the baby. What would you do if you had car trouble?"

In reality, he was paranoid the entire time I was gone from the house. When I returned, he interrogated me about the places I went and the people I saw.

Though I never gave him a reason to distrust me, he did.

And then I had another baby and another baby. At that point, I stopped thinking about running away, much less trying to escape. Tommy told me repeatedly, "If you ever try to leave me, I'll kill you, and I'll kill your family." Early on he meant my mom, Nana, and extended family—but before long, his threats included even our own children. Whenever Tommy turned violent, my first thought was to protect our kids.

CHAPTER 9

Trapped

I didn't understand that the longer I remained in my marriage with Tommy, the tougher it would be to escape his abuse. I had always assumed I could leave at any time. But with each addition to our family, Tommy's control over me intensified.

On February 26, 1993, Timothy Joel, our second son, entered our lives. This precious dark-haired baby was born during the annual camp meeting services held at our church. Camp meeting was a busy time for all the Schankweilers, as our congregation hosted services with special guest speakers and musicians three times a day for an entire week.

Perhaps because my due date was near—a mere week away—I was especially sensitive and emotional during camp meeting that year. I attended services every day and evening and enjoyed listening to Pastor Paul Lucas, the white-haired speaker who told riveting stories from his past about how God had brought him through various difficulties. Sitting in the front row of the church, I hung on his every word and drank in the message the man of God spoke. His voice was strong and authoritative, but his heart was tender and soft. He wore a long suit coat with a flowing tie. His demeanor reminded me of the sort of presence I thought Abraham or Moses must have had in biblical times.

Listening to Pastor Lucas tell how God had delivered him from a terrible past stirred hope in me that God could do something similar for my husband. My heart was thumping with excitement, and I didn't want to miss a single service.

A couple of days into the camp meeting, I went to a previously scheduled appointment with my doctor. "Have you felt the baby move in the past twenty-four hours?" he asked.

"No, I haven't," I replied. The doctor sent me to the hospital for a stress test, but by the time we reached the hospital, my labor had begun and a few hours later that evening, a second baby boy joined our family. We named him Timothy Joel—two biblical names. He was gorgeous with a perfectly round face, dark hair, and piercing blue eyes. I was twenty-one years old and holding my second baby boy. My heart was so full as I stared into Timothy's eyes.

I felt good enough after the birth, so within forty-eight hours, I slipped into the back row of the church holding baby Timothy to my breast. I sat and listened to Paul Lucas deliver his final message to end camp meeting that year. Tommy went with me but decided we should leave before the conclusion of the service.

My world revolved around our two little boys, and my goal was to be the best mother and wife I could be. I thought if I could be a better wife and mom, Tommy might be better too.

He didn't make it easy. He continued to excoriate me for my inabilities. Whether it was cooking, cleaning, or even taking care of the baby, Tommy showed me the "correct" way to do everything. "You learned it wrong," he said. I struggled with feelings that I was never good enough no matter what I did or how hard I tried.

"Go talk to my mom so she can show you the right way to do things," Tommy told me.

Oddly enough, I had never struggled with a lack of confidence prior to my marriage. I knew I was loved by my family members and liked by my friends. I enjoyed dance classes of all genres, including ballet, tap, jazz, and even clogging! For a while I took modeling classes and participated in several fashion shows for department stores. My family reinforced my positive self-image, often telling me, "You are smart. You are funny! You are beautiful." Most importantly, I felt Mom and Dad's love, so I never questioned my ability to be successful at whatever I chose to do.

But after nearly eighteen years of my family encouraging me to feel secure, happy, and positive about life, Tommy destroyed those attributes in less than eighteen months, pulverizing any positive attitudes I had about myself into oblivion. I felt trapped in a prison of Tommy's making.

Perhaps worse yet, I allowed him to do it.

CHAPTER 10

Hidden Bruises, Unseen Wounds

Well into our third year of marriage—with two babies, lots of bills, and even more secrets—I continued to love my husband regardless of his bad behavior. I was determined to keep our young family together. Although I knew now that Tommy was a controlling, short-tempered man, I felt I was doing the right thing by believing for the best, despite the obvious.

But on a good day, when Tommy's mood was upbeat, he was a fun, likable guy. He had a great sense of humor and often responded to situations with a funny remark or quip that caused everyone who heard him to crack up laughing. When Tommy was "up," his vibrant personality attracted people. They enjoyed his company and his infectious energy. His enthusiasm for the outdoors combined with a bit of a daredevil spirit spurred numerous adventures for himself and friends. He loved action and wanted to be in the center of it.

All of that made Tommy a popular person in our circles. He was well-known throughout Avon Park, mainly because of Pastor Schankweiler's influence in the community. Many of the church folks had known Tommy since he was a little boy. Later, as a young man, Tommy worked alongside his dad, helping to construct many of the homes in the neighborhoods making up the church compound. The congregation saw Tommy as an extension of his father and assumed the best about him.

As had I. I genuinely liked the version of Tommy with whom I fell in love as a teenager. He had many good qualities, and we laughed a lot in the early days of our marriage. He had an especially creative mind, and his skills at fixing mechanical things gave me a certain sense of security. I never worried about one of our vehicles breaking down because I knew Tommy could repair almost anything. Same with household appliances. We never called a repairman if something malfunctioned. Tommy studied how the thing was supposed to work, and then he fixed it.

His talent for woodworking was exceptional as well. I sometimes accompanied him as he shopped for just the right pieces of lumber with which he would construct handmade furniture for our home. He was truly amazing and probably could have been successful at anything he attempted to do. Unfortunately, that did not include working on our marriage.

Tommy's temper grew more virulent, and his violent, erratic rages became standard fare around our house. I rarely physically fought back against Tommy anymore, because I realized that the harder I struggled against him, the worse injuries I'd suffer. Often I'd be sore and achy for days after one of our fights. I attempted to conceal my bruises by wearing several layers of clothes. Nobody else could see the welts and discolored hematomas on my body, but I could sure feel them.

I felt as though I was walking on eggshells all the time. One day Tommy got upset about something and we were fighting. Before I knew it, he had shot a gun in my direction. The bullet went all the way through the side of our trailer and exited through the exterior siding of the house. "I wasn't trying to hit you," he said. "If I wanted to shoot you, I wouldn't have missed. I just wanted to get your attention." That was one of Tommy's ways of controlling me. Eventually I put a picture over the hole in the wall.

Before then, however, my parents and older stepbrother, Gary, visited. Gary noticed the bullet hole in the siding of the double-wide and nodded toward it. "Why is there a bullet hole in your siding?" he asked. "What's that about?"

"Oh, that's nothing," I said, waving my hand toward the front of the house, brushing off his question. "Tommy was cleaning his gun and it went off."

Gary didn't say much. He just nodded. "Uh-huh," he said.

I knew he didn't believe me. I cringed inside, not merely because I was lying to my stepbrother, but also because this was another potential opportunity to involve someone else in what could've been an intervention with Tommy.

But instead I lied and covered for my husband—again.

CHAPTER 11

Goodbye, Nana

As Tommy's power over me increased, he grew less comfortable with me taking trips to Tampa to visit my family. If Nana wanted to go, however, Tommy reluctantly tolerated me being gone from home. Nana and I made the trip about once a month for several successive months, and we always enjoyed our time together, excitedly talking about all sorts of girly things as well as spiritual truths she wanted me to know. Normally, I took the two baby boys along with me, and Nana loved pampering them. I appreciated her help, too, as her attention on the boys gave me a bit of a break.

On one of the trips to Tampa, Nana confided as she was driving, "I've been having headaches for several days now. Would you please get me some Tylenol from my purse?"

"Certainly," I said. "I'll be glad to. But are you sure you feel like going to Tampa, Nana?" I understood that Nana, an experienced nurse, knew her body, but I didn't want her to travel if she didn't feel well. On the other hand, since we were halfway there, it would take equally as long to get back home as it would to arrive in Tampa.

"Oh, I'm fine," she said. Nana took the medication, and we continued driving.

Despite Nana's discomfort, we enjoyed a fabulous time together. We went to the mall before we met up with the rest of our family, and Nana bought Timmy a little green squeaky frog. She also purchased a special bottle of perfume for me. She knew Tommy and I were on a tight budget, and I couldn't afford such a luxury. She loved making me feel pretty, so she showered me with special love-gifts every chance she could.

"Thank you so much, Nana," I said as I hugged her. "And guess what? I just found out I'm pregnant again!"

Nana was ecstatic. "Oh, Sandee Jo!" She nearly shrieked with joy in the department store. "That is such good news. And this one is going to be our little girl. I just know it!"

"I really hope so, Nana," I replied.

We left the mall and went to visit with my great-grandparents and my mom. I appreciated time with my mom more than ever, even if it was only for a day. And Mom was thrilled to have the chance to spoil the boys with love and kindness. She relished playing with them all afternoon. All too soon, it was time for me to head back to Avon Park. Nana planned to stay a few extra days, so I packed up the babies' things, hugged and kissed everyone, and was on my way before dark.

I had barely gotten home when my mom called. I thought she wanted to gush over her time with the babies, but I was wrong. "Sandee Jo, I need to tell you something," she said. Her voice sounded serious.

"Sure, Mom, what's going on?"

"Nana's in the hospital. She suffered a massive brain aneurysm tonight and has slipped into a coma."

"No!" I screamed into the telephone. "That can't be. We enjoyed a beautiful day together. She was fine this afternoon." And then I remembered her headaches. I couldn't help wondering if I should have done something differently, something that might have prevented her from having an aneurysm. I knew better, but the thoughts still nagged at me.

Nana never made it back to Avon Park. She hung on for a few more days, and then she was gone. She was only sixty-one years of age.

I was shattered. She was the one piece of my life that was grounded, the person I leaned on the most; she was an extension of my mom, whom I missed terribly since moving away. In a town where I knew few people, Nana lived just down the street if I needed something. She was the one to whom I could talk.

Even after the ugly incident she'd observed with Tommy, she stuck by me. I think she would have been okay with me leaving him, but she knew I had to make my own decisions. Even if they were wrong or unwise, she chose to love me through my choices.

A rush of memories flooded over me. Most of those memories involved life with Nana long before she had introduced me to Tommy. I recalled that my brother and I had spent parts of our summers with Nana and Grandpa Terry at their building site, where they planned and built their own home on one of Florida's many lakes. Grandpa Terry was an architect by trade, and he designed the house from top to bottom. Billy and I watched him build it, and even helped whenever he allowed us to. I remembered handing Grandpa tile squares as he carefully put the finishing touches on one of the bathrooms, as Nana supervised.

When the home was completed, we spent our summers swimming and waterskiing on the lake behind Nana and Grandpa Terry's home. Then each year, as the summer slipped away, Nana took us shopping for school supplies at one of the stores in Avon Park.

Now she was gone, and I was mourning her loss alone in that same small town.

Tommy offered condolences, but mostly he seemed irritated that I couldn't control my tears, that my heart was broken, and that

I needed comfort to deal with Nana's death. To him, it all seemed like a huge inconvenience that I was weeping all the time, grieving to the point I felt numb, and unable to give our babies the attention they needed.

"It's your job to be strong and hold it together," Tommy told me.

It annoyed Tommy to see me cry. Even during arguments and fights, I had learned to hold back my tears because the sight of them made Tommy even angrier than he already was.

But now my tears flowed freely. I could no longer prevent them from streaming down my face. Nor did I try. I hurt so deeply and longed to be held and comforted by my husband. He seemed incapable of comprehending that, much less doing it.

Although Nana was not there to greet her, our little girl arrived on November 7, 1994. We named her Tonie Joanne. I wanted to honor my grandmother and to have a bit of Nana live on through our daughter. We would connect the Jo to her first name, similar to how my family had connected Jo to my first name. At the time, it didn't occur to me that our family names sounded like those on the 1960s sitcom *Petticoat Junction*!

Tonie Jo brought me so much joy the moment I saw her. Almost instantly, the huge hole in my heart left by Nana's departure became much smaller. I felt Nana smiling at Tonie Jo and me from heaven. Our precious baby girl came at a time when God knew I needed fresh air breathed into my soul. Without a doubt, God drew me much closer to Him and hugged me warmly in the form of our fragile, perfect baby girl.

⚭

Nearly a year later, my family gathered in Tampa for our first Mother's Day without Nana. During the trip to Tampa, with our kids along with us, the air-conditioning stopped working in our old car. It was May in Florida, and the children were hot, cranky, and miserable, and so were Tommy and I. Sadness overwhelmed me.

Tommy began yelling at me in the car because he was irritated about the circumstances—as if I had any control over the situation!

I felt helpless and was too despondent to even argue back. I just let him yell, but I couldn't believe he insisted on inflicting even more pain at a time like this by screaming at me.

So I didn't respond. In truth, I couldn't. I was so far removed from myself that day, I found it impossible to worry about what Tommy wanted.

Not surprisingly, what Tommy wanted was for us to go home. Immediately after the Mother's Day celebration, Tommy grunted to me, "Come on. Let's go."

I wanted to linger amid the comfort of my family. I wanted to hug my mom a little longer—especially now that her mom was gone. I wanted to cry a few more tears with my special aunts and reminisce about what a marvelous woman my grandmother was… but no. Tommy didn't like seeing me in the presence of my family for too long. He did not want to chance losing control of me. So he made up an excuse that we had to leave and ripped me away from my family.

The drive back seemed interminable. I don't recall saying a word.

But as we neared Avon Park, the reality hit me: I would never see Nana again until heaven. No longer would I be encouraged by her soft, warm smile. Nor would I hear her sweet voice calling me Sissy. I would never again feel the comfort of her arms around me. Nana was no longer a phone call away, and my emotions overwhelmed me.

I tried unsuccessfully to hide my grief, knowing Tommy would be displeased if he detected my emotions on display. He would not allow for such weakness. But I had been stifling my grief since the moment I learned Nana was gone, and my own body would no longer permit the strain. Sitting in the passenger seat of the car as Tommy drove, I doubled over, unable to breathe. For several seconds I gasped for breath, then a deep, loud, guttural wail bellowed out of me. It was as though my heart was bursting right there in the passenger seat. Tears surged out of me like a flood current breaking through a dam. My inconsolable condition took Tommy aback.

Suddenly, he pulled the car off the road and reached over toward me. I felt his hand on my back, patting me like he might a small child...or a dog. He continued softly patting me in silence for several minutes. He said nothing.

After a few more minutes, I sat up and wiped the tears from my swollen eyes. Tommy put the car in gear, and we finished the ride home in awkward silence. He never brought up the matter again, nor did he attempt to console me in any other way. I grieved the loss of Nana alone. Sadly, I expected nothing more from Tommy.

CHAPTER 12

Juiced!

*I*t was difficult to deal with the unexpected twists and turns, ups and downs of Tommy's anger issues. Trying to predict and avoid triggers that might cause my husband to snap was like trying to predict the path of an active tornado. It was impossible to know for sure in which direction he might lash out once everything began swirling around us.

On one occasion when Timmy was barely a year old and toddling around the house, three-year-old Bubba was tempting his baby brother to touch a lightbulb in a lamp. I saw what was going on and said, "No, Bubba. Don't do that. That lightbulb is hot."

Just then, Tommy came into the room and heard me rebuking Bubba. "Do you think that's funny?" he growled at Bubba. "Do you want your little brother to get burned?"

Tommy unscrewed the still hot lightbulb and looked at Bubba. "Come here, boy!" he yelled. "I'll show you how hot this is."

"No…" Bubba cried, cowering away from his dad.

"Come here, boy!" Tommy roared.

Bubba slowly stepped over to his dad, and when he was within arm's reach, Tommy took the hot lightbulb and pressed the glass to Bubba's cheek.

"Don't do that!" I told Tommy, but I was too late. Bubba wailed in pain as the heat from the hot bulb seared his skin, leaving a red burn.

"That'll teach him," Tommy said to me. That sort of treatment was Tommy's idea of discipline. He scoffed at the idea of a time-out. He would huff, "You don't get your kid to obey by giving 'em a time-out."

Usually he held himself in check fairly well when we were around his parents or mine. In front of our parents, he'd simply snap his fingers at the boys and say, "You'd better straighten up." But occasionally he let down his guard and revealed his true nature. That's what happened during Tonie Jo's first road trip with us, when she was a mere two weeks old. We were traveling to Pennsylvania to visit with Tommy's family prior to Thanksgiving.

Visiting Tommy's extended family members was always a pleasant experience for us. A large, kind, loving family full of life and energy, Tommy's relatives all seemed to possess excellent gifts of hospitality. Despite the frigid Pennsylvania temperatures, Tommy's family welcomed us warmly, making us feel special and right at home.

When all the aunts, uncles, and cousins gathered to enjoy the holiday together, the house was filled with fun and laughter. While the men of the family went hunting, the women gathered to cook, bake, eat, and catch up with each other, as the little ones played together with cousins they seldom got to see.

As Thanksgiving approached, I was actually looking forward to being with Tommy's extended family up north. But because I knew the first holiday without Nana would be emotionally tough for my mom, I didn't want her to be alone when her heart was still hurting at that time of year.

"What would you think about my mom going along with us to Pennsylvania for Thanksgiving?" I asked Tommy. "She could help with the kids along the way, and it would be good for her to be with your family."

"Sure, why not?" Tommy said with a shrug. "What's one more person with that bunch?"

I knew such a move would be risky, since long road trips seemed to be a breeding ground for Tommy's disrespect, disenchantments, and disagreements. Almost anything could set him off. He didn't like to hear the baby cry; he hated making stops for bathroom breaks any more than necessary; everything about travel by truck or car seemed to irritate him.

Still, I couldn't stand the idea of Mom staying in Tampa for her first Thanksgiving without Nana, so I felt the risk was worth it. Moreover, I knew Tommy could control his temper when he wanted to. Yes, he experienced mood swings, but many of his actions were intentional and calculated. He was like a light switch, turning anger on and off according to the circumstances, so I hoped he would realize how important it was for my mom to join us for this trip and control his temper in front of her.

When I invited Mom to go with us, she was delighted. She looked forward to spending time with her three grandchildren, and I was excited to spend some pleasant time with her.

We made the long trip from Florida to Pennsylvania without incident. We enjoyed a delightful Thanksgiving with Tommy's extended family members and stayed a few extra days after the holiday so Tommy could go hunting with the guys. Then we loaded up the truck and headed back home.

We were making good time when, about three-quarters of the way home, we stopped for gas and some food. Everything was going well until Mom, after grabbing something to eat, delayed a little longer than Tommy deemed necessary. As Tommy, Bubba, Timmy, Tonie Jo, and I sat in the truck outside the restaurant, I could tell Tommy was fuming. He spewed a litany of rude things about my mom, right in front of the kids.

"Tommy, we are almost home," I pleaded. "Please don't make a scene." I should have known better.

The moment my mom got into the back seat of the truck, Tommy made a snide remark about how long it had taken her in the bathroom.

Mom, of course, was unaware of Tommy's volatile personality—but never one to back down from a confrontation, she fired a sarcastic comment right back at him. I had long since stopped snapping back at Tommy during our conflicts because I knew my responses only made matters worse.

Tommy had been on good behavior the entire trip and had gone for several days without a single incident. But he was not accustomed to being challenged by a woman in his own truck. He had been drinking from a large container of orange juice, and when Mom returned insult for insult, Tommy whirled around in his seat and hurled his orange juice directly at my mom, hitting her right in the face and hair. The sticky liquid dripped down her face and clothes, then spread out onto the truck's seat.

"Aghhh!" she yelled, then peeled out of the truck and stormed back into the restaurant.

I was furious with Tommy and let him know it. "I can't believe you did that!" I hollered at him so loudly, I scared the kids. I knew I would pay dearly for my outburst, but at that moment, I didn't care what he did to me. It didn't matter. I could not believe he had been so recklessly rude to my mother.

The children had witnessed some of Tommy's despicable behavior previously, but my mother never had seen anyone but good and charming Tommy. Now she had gotten a taste of the truth.

After another ten or fifteen minutes went by, she returned to the truck and announced to all of us, but primarily to Tommy, "I'll find my own way home, thank you."

Tommy immediately shifted into damage control, apologizing all over himself. "Oh, no, please. You don't need to do that. I'm so sorry. I didn't mean to do that. Please, please forgive me."

Mom paid no attention and continued reaching into the vehicle, gathering her bags and belongings. Tommy kept apologizing and asking for forgiveness all the while, and tears even trickled from his eyes.

Whatever he said or did worked. When Mom saw Tommy's tears, she melted and consented to ride the rest of the way to Florida with us. Tommy flashed me a look, as though to say, "See? Even your mom can be fooled." I glared back at him in silence. Before long, we were back on the road.

I should have sided with my mom when she said she was leaving. I should have gathered the children and left him right there. Over the ensuing years, I wished I had walked away a million times or more. But I didn't.

Although Tommy's outlandish actions had cast a shadow on our otherwise bright and cheerful vacation, Mom dismissed his childish behavior as an isolated incident brought on by travel fatigue.

Both Tommy and I knew otherwise, and three young children in the back were learning the truth as well.

CHAPTER 13

Medicating the Madness

A s we moved into our fifth year of marriage, I saw no feasible way of escaping Tommy's unpredictable behavior without enormous risk to our children, me, and possibly others, including Tommy himself. His threats became increasingly more ominous and more real. He was no longer merely spouting menacing words but declaring more elaborately thought-out plans of action.

I had run out of excuses for Tommy's behavior, so although he refused to return to the marriage counselor suggested by his parents, he was at least willing to see a doctor to help him manage what his physician described as bipolar disorder. The doctor recommended a therapist, and to my surprise, Tommy consented to an appointment. Then another and another.

The therapist confirmed the bipolar disorder and prescribed medication for Tommy. The meds helped but did not cure anything. Worse yet, the diagnosis gave Tommy an excuse for his abusive behavior—a label he wore around like an Olympian's gold medal.

Now fights that once ended with apologies instead ended with him crassly declaring, "I can't control my actions. Don't you know I have bipolar disorder? I'm not to blame." He repeatedly reminded me, "I have a clinical diagnosis, and my behavior is a symptom!"

He blamed his surly behavior on everything from "I forgot to take my medicine" to "The doctor prescribed the wrong dosage" to "These meds cause me to blow up as a side effect." And of course he blamed his bad behavior on me. "It's your fault. If you were a better wife and mother, I wouldn't get so angry." Any excuse would do now that Tommy had an ally in his diagnosis. It was far easier for him to blame somebody or something else than to take responsibility for his actions.

Tommy's doctors played right into his hands, unwittingly making matters worse by providing him a list of common behaviors sometimes exhibited by patients suffering from bipolar conditions. Once Tommy had that sort of ammunition readily at his disposal, he stopped trying to control his temper. Rather than attempting to discover why he acted as he did and bettering himself through counseling and medication, he simply used the diagnosis as a crutch, a free pass for his terrible behavior.

Tommy's diagnosis came with a whole list of medications, but he was not willing to sort them out. That was my job, he said. I was responsible for making sure his prescriptions were filled and that his doctors' appointments flowed seamlessly to avoid lapses in his receiving the proper treatments. I did my best to help, but sometimes I lost track between taking care of the children and working outside the home at a daycare center. When Tommy missed a medication, that was a license to do whatever he wanted. Then, of course, he blamed his violent actions on the absence of medications, which he emphasized was *my* fault, not his. "You'd better not forget next time," he warned. He implied that the whole family would suffer if I failed to keep up.

I felt sure that some nightmare was inevitable in the future of our marriage. I assumed that someday I might not walk away from one of our fights, that I'd be either permanently maimed or dead. Our fights seemed to get more out of control, each one leaving me in worse condition than the previous. I could easily imagine that one day, when he shoved me, my head would crash against a piece of furniture and render me unconscious or worse. Or that Tommy might wrench his tightly gripped hands around my throat a little too long, choking me to death. The dark methods of doom played in my mind and caused me to worry how my kids might function without a mom. Tommy had already made it known to me that if I should die, that would be the end of our kids' relationships with my family members. "I'll cut that off right there," he threatened.

Once, after another intense argument had escalated into a fierce fight, I took time to write out my wishes for the children should Tommy kill me. I jotted down everything I could think of concerning my children and with whom I preferred them placed if I died young. I said, "I want my kids to have a relationship with my mom and with our family." I wasn't bold enough to write straightforwardly, "If I am found dead, it will likely be because of my husband." But I hoped the reader would catch my drift. I folded the paper and sealed it in an envelope. I hid it deep in the kitchen cupboard for several months, where it could easily be discovered but in a location where I didn't think Tommy would look. Then one day, to my horror, Tommy was searching for something and started going through the kitchen cupboards and drawers. He came within inches of finding the letter. After that, I worried that Tommy might find the letter before he killed me, then circumvent my wishes—so I destroyed the note I had written. I never wrote another.

Tommy was an intelligent man. He knew just how and where to hit me to inflict the most pain while leaving the least amount of evidence for others around us—namely his parents or mine— to notice. Even in the heat of a raging argument, he was careful that when he struck me, his blows landed in areas covered by my clothing. After these beatings, he forced me to keep any bruises on my arms and legs hidden. Some people in the church congregation probably thought I was trying to dress "more holy." On the contrary, I feared for my life and for the lives of our children should anyone close to us truly understand what the preacher's son was doing at home.

If he didn't pummel my body, Tommy usually hit me in my head, not my face. Sometimes he yanked my hair so forcefully, I ached with a stiff neck for days afterward. My head throbbed horribly from him pulling out my hair. At times he might yank out entire handfuls. It hurt so severely afterward, I couldn't slide a soft brush through my hair without flinching in pain.

Throughout this unstable marriage, I managed to maintain my relationship with God. I always felt that He heard my prayers and my cries for help, so I continued to pray, even through the darkest hours. I sensed a real security through prayer, even though at times I was confused as to why God would allow the abuse to happen. I sometimes got angry with God when it seemed He didn't hear me, or at least did not respond the way I had hoped. Still, I prayed. Although I often felt helpless in my situation, I never felt hopeless.

During this entire time, Tommy, the kids, and I continued to attend church services regularly. Our congregation had grown in number, and our church property now included a private Christian school as well as a daycare center. I worked at both, in addition to helping at the church.

Tommy and I drove the church bus, picking up children and adults on Sunday mornings and Wednesday evenings. Tommy also helped teach the high school teenagers at the church, and they loved him. Serving at the church was rewarding, and it lifted my spirits to be involved in doing something so worthwhile. Moreover, church attendance was the one consistently positive element in the life of our family. Even though Tommy's mood fluctuated at home and he experienced multiple mental meltdowns, he continued to attend church with us, no doubt because his dad was the pastor. Maybe he had an earnest desire to draw closer to God, or possibly he attended out of guilt. He often responded to invitations at church to repent of his sins, and I was convinced he was sincere. He was never too specific about why he had responded, couching his need in vague language such as, "I'm having some spiritual struggles." Sometimes we responded together to pray, and a number of people from the congregation gathered around us, praying aloud. We'd pray until Pap would ask, "Is every heart clear?"

I had high hopes that Tommy was turning a corner, that he would change as a result of this special time of prayer. I hoped that his repentance was the start of something new, that he would value himself and me as well. Unfortunately, that didn't happen.

Regardless, I was glad he went with us. The church provided a sense of stability and a place where I felt the kids and I were safe.

CHAPTER 14

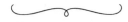

Pet Cemetery

When our daughter Tonie Jo was three years old, we moved across the field. We were only a short distance away from Tommy's mom and dad, with an orange grove between us. We were still close to the church compound since we rented an old farmhouse from Granny and Pap that included a bit of property. The house sat off the road and had a long, winding, picturesque driveway, which was lined with large trees. The yard was graced by a big, beautiful oak tree with a tire swing hanging down within easy reach for the kids. The house, located near a lake, had a wraparound porch overlooking a large backyard where the kids could play. Everything about the property looked peaceful and inviting.

The home was old but spacious inside. The boys shared a large bedroom, with plenty of space for their Tonka trucks and Legos. Tonie Jo had her own room, which I decorated with plenty of pink and pretty pictures on her wall, reflecting her role as the princess in our family of five.

Our move to the larger house breathed fresh air into our marriage, but it was short-lived. Tommy continued to treat the children and me horribly. My husband gave me many reasons to hate him over the years, but one of the most heartrending was his penchant for killing the children's pets.

Now that we had more property, Tommy allowed the kids to have a female potbellied pig as a pet. The kids named her Cheerio, and Tommy built a small pen for her just off our back porch. Tommy wanted the kids—Bubba, age six, Timmy, age four, and Tonie Jo, who was three years old—to learn responsibility, so it was their job to care for the animal. They had to feed Cheerio, keep her supplied with fresh water (no small task when keeping a pig hydrated), and clean her pen each day.

Apparently, Cheerio was pregnant when we got her, because within a few months, she gave birth to a number of little piglets. "All the more reason to make sure the water bowls are filled," Tommy reminded the children regularly.

But the kids were young and having fun playing outside in the yard, and they often forgot to water the pigs. I tried to cover for them, often checking to make sure the pigs had water, but I sometimes forgot as well.

Tommy found the pigs' bowls empty several times and warned the boys, "Do not let that happen."

And for a while the boys diligently obeyed their dad. But the boys didn't always remember, and the pigs didn't always move in the daintiest of fashion, so the water often spilled, resulting in some empty bowls.

When I heard Tommy outside yelling at the boys, I could almost guess what had happened and knew they were in trouble. I ran outside just as Tommy yelled, "The pigs' water dish is empty again! So to teach you a lesson, I'm going to kill the pig." He glared at Bubba and Timmy. "And *you* will watch me do it."

Cheerio squealed and squirmed as Tommy grabbed the pig by her feet and dragged her out of the pen.

Declaring he was teaching the kids a lesson for not properly caring for their animals, Tommy forced us to stand and watch as he abruptly murdered the animal right in front of the children and me. He shot Cheerio right in the head. The kids immediately started crying, while Tommy walked back to the pen and shot each one of the piglets as well.

The kids were devastated, but Tommy didn't seem to care. He had no emotional attachment to the animals, even though he liked the energy a new pet brought to our home. Tommy always relished the hero role at the beginning of procuring a pet. He helped pick out the animal, purchased supplies for it, and built a pen for it. But after the newness wore off, Tommy lost patience quickly, both with the pet and with the children's inability to maintain it. One pet after another died at his cruel hands. On one occasion, Tommy shoved a ferret up the tailpipe of his vehicle. On another, the despot demanded that our young daughter skin her pet rabbit with a knife, after which he cooked it.

These sporadic acts of brutality usually occurred on a whim, when Tommy decided the pet was making too much noise or perhaps had an accident inside the house. Regardless of the reason, Tommy always had the final say, and often, without warning, he decided it was time for a pet to die. Most died with bullet holes in their heads. That was Tommy's way of dealing with things that annoyed him—and the message was not lost on me.

Pets were a bittersweet diversion around our house. They brought joy to the kids, but they also brought grief. Tommy's violence was a means to control everyone. If you loved a pet, you were vulnerable. He killed my precious dog, Mandie, with a bow and arrow shot straight through the heart. Tommy then took me door-to-door in our neighborhood to ask if anyone had seen Mandie, knowing the entire time that he had killed our dog.

In another incident, Tommy was mad about something, so he took Timothy's dog, grabbed it by the tail, and slammed it to the concrete sidewalk. The dog limped off into the woods, and Timothy witnessed the whole thing.

That was how Tommy maintained his vise-grip of control. If the children or I fell in love with a pet, he used it as leverage to dominate us, usually by killing the pet.

But killing the children's pets wasn't the only way the kids suffered Tommy's wrath. He beat and spanked our boys, Bubba and Timothy, with a vengeance. They were tough and took it.

The treatment Tommy gave our daughter Tonie Jo was more emotionally and mentally abusive. For instance, as she grew into a preteen, she was a real overachiever; whatever she did, she put her heart and soul into it. She wanted to be a doctor from the time she was six years old. Yet Tommy put her down all the time. One day when she was about twelve years old, he said to her, "Make me a glass of tea and fix me a sandwich."

She hurried to the kitchen and made some tea as he sat at the table waiting for her to serve him.

Just as she put his tea and sandwich down on the table, she spilled some tea. Tommy looked at her with disdain and said, "Are you kidding me? And *you* wanna be a doctor?" He rolled his eyes and snarled. "Do you really think you're gonna be a surgeon? With those clumsy hands? Go get me another glass of tea."

She took away the tea and brought him another full glass, but I could tell she was devastated. I was exasperated and thought, *How could he have done that to his daughter?* But he heaped similar demeaning comments on our children all the time. It was as though he felt bad about himself, so he wanted everyone else to feel bad about themselves as well.

CHAPTER 15

The Near-Deadly 911 Call

Tommy had often threatened me, "If you ever call the police, I'll kill everybody." I honestly believed that he would. And because he had been a corrections officer, he boasted, "I'll never spend any time in jail." Whether he thought the authorities would be lenient on him or that he could beat the system, I wasn't sure. But I knew he would not be deterred by fear of reprisal or prison time.

Although I often wanted to call the police during the first eight years of our marriage, I never did. Mostly I didn't call for help because I feared what Tommy might do to the children and me the moment the police left our home. Even if they apprehended Tommy and took him to jail, I could imagine him being freed within a few days and then coming back home angrier than ever. And what if I *did* manage to pack up the kids and run? I knew it would be only a matter of time before he found us. Or if he couldn't find us, he'd retaliate against my family members, as he had often threatened to do.

Tommy clearly stated his intentions. "If you ever call the police and they come to our house, I will shoot them on the spot. Then I will shoot the kids and you," he declared, looking me straight in the eyes. "And then I'll finish by killing myself. I will never spend time behind bars."

More and more, Tommy told me, "I hate myself, and I have nothing to live for."

Whether his words were bluff or bluster, I believed Tommy would follow through on his threats. Consequently, I never called the police for help.

But on the cold first day of February 1998, while the kids were at their grandparents' home, Tommy's outburst took the form of building a fire in a barrel outside. He placed it near the porch and threw items from the house into it—namely *my* things. When I didn't respond the way he anticipated, Tommy angrily grabbed a chain saw. When I eluded him, he came stomping through our dining room, and with the chain saw buzzing loudly, he cut up our table and chairs, slice by slice. He hauled pieces out to the barrel behind our house and set the wood on fire.

Tommy knew I loved that crafted table and collection of chairs—a unique set that he himself had carved by hand—but my mistake was letting him know that I cared for it. Loving something made it a target. Next he went after my photo albums, including special pictures of my nana.

I was hiding from him when I heard the noise coming from an area of the house where I kept my most treasured items—poetry books, special awards, and my photo albums. I had one album packed full of pictures of special memories with Nana during our summers together when I was a little girl. I also had albums of high school trips and family trips all carefully assembled and captioned.

I ran toward Tommy with desperation in my eyes. I sensed what he intended to do, so I latched onto him as tightly as I could hold him, trying to interrupt his steps, but he shrugged me off and proceeded toward the door to my treasures. I cried out to him,

"Tommy! Please, please don't do it. I'll do whatever you want. Just don't do this."

But Tommy smelled weakness in the air. He knew he had found an area of vulnerability in my wanting to protect the family photos, which must have made him even more determined to destroy what I deemed precious. He grabbed several of the photo albums, lugged them outside, and threw them into the fire. The blaze leaped higher as it consumed my family photos in seconds, turning them to ashes in the barrel.

In a desperate attempt to interrupt his rampage, I grabbed Tommy's favorite cowboy hat, ran outside, and tossed it into the fire too. He'd worn that hat in a rodeo, and it was one thing he seemed to genuinely care about. I knew my impulsive action would evoke a response from Tommy, and it did—immediately.

He chased me through the house, grabbing at me ferociously. When he caught me, his strong hands latched onto my hair. With horrendous force, he yanked me around the floor, dragging me from one room to another, my body slamming against the doorways. As I struggled wildly to get free, I thought to myself, *I'm not sure I'm going to make it out of this.* Tommy pounced on me and struck me again and again with powerful blows all over my upper body. I screamed and begged for him to stop, and with me barely conscious, he finally relented. I lay on the floor in pain, afraid for my life.

When I heard him leave the room, I crawled to the telephone and dialed 911. Tommy must have heard me because he burst back into the room. I quickly hung up without speaking a word into the phone, but he tore the phone from the wall.

Even though I had not had time to express my emergency to the 911 operator, Tommy must have guessed the police would respond regardless—and they did. A few minutes later, from our front windows, he spotted their police cruiser winding down the long lane to our driveway. He grabbed a rifle before hiding against the wall behind the door in our bedroom. "Get rid of them," he growled. "Make them go away, or I will start shooting and won't stop until everyone is dead, including me."

He stayed concealed where he could see the front door and the police officers, but they could not see him. He hoisted the loaded rifle, ready to fire.

The officers knocked on the front door, and Tommy nodded toward me to answer it. I slowly opened the door, knowing Tommy was observing my every move with his finger on the trigger.

One of the officers said, "We received a call from the 911 operator, and we're following up on it. Is everything okay?"

"Oh, yes," I said. "Everything's fine. It must have been an accident, a misdial." I tried to make eye contact with the officer and somehow convey to him that I was scared to death, but he didn't seem to notice the desperation in my eyes. Instead he kept looking over my shoulder, past me and into the house.

"Whatcha got burnin' back there?" he asked.

"Oh, just some odds and ends," I lied. "My husband has been burning some trash."

"All right," the officer said. "Sorry to bother you." The two policemen turned and walked back to their squad car, and as I watched them drive away, my heart plunged further into despair. I closed the door, knowing I had just missed a golden opportunity to escape. My help had come and gone.

Years later I learned the officers had reported the incident as: "a suspicious incident, unfounded." Tommy launched back into beating me with even more vengeance than before. He was determined to make me pay for calling the police. He pounded my upper body, my arms, and my head.

Although my eye was blackened to a deep purple and blue, I was glad Tommy missed punching me in my belly. A few weeks later, I learned that baby number four had been tucked inside me during Tommy's rage.

I breathed a sigh of relief that the baby was okay, but I never again called the police for help.

CHAPTER 16

Why Did I Stay?
Why Didn't I Tell?

Why didn't I tell anyone about what was going on in our marriage? Why didn't I reach out to anyone for help? Most puzzling, why did I stay in that relationship after I discovered the violence Tommy was capable of inflicting upon me, then later upon our children as well? Those are questions I grappled with then, and I still do to this day.

I truly believed I loved him—and I think I did at first—so I told myself what I wanted to hear: *No husband is perfect. He must be stressed. After all, he's a hard worker. He won't do such a thing again.* Or worse yet: *Maybe it really is my fault.* I knew that even the best relationships had ups and downs, fun times and difficult days.

I did not want our marriage to end in divorce, as so many marriages in my family had done. Moreover, nobody in Tommy's family had ever divorced, as Tommy often reminded me. "Schankweilers don't divorce," he said. I didn't know if that was a promise or a threat.

Perhaps most confusing of all, I convinced myself that Tommy was sorry after he beat me. He always cried and seemed remorseful after his outbursts of temper. He often prayed for God's forgiveness and for His help in controlling his anger. Tommy apologized frequently to me and seemed sincere after each episode. Then his eyes would well with tears. "I'm so sorry. I don't know why I did that," he'd sob. "I…I just don't understand."

And I'd forgive him again.

His aggression seemed to pass as quickly as it flared. When our emotions settled after the fight, Tommy would express his love for me. Even though Tommy was an extremely controlling and short-tempered man, I wanted to keep our family together. I truly believed God wanted us to stay together too.

I was especially conflicted when, ten days before our ninth wedding anniversary, I gave birth to a beautiful baby girl on October 11, 1998. We named her Tayler Jewell. Despite the chaos and craziness in our marriage, when I gazed into the face of that darling baby, I gave thanks to God.

By this point, barring a miracle, I no longer held much hope that Tommy would change and that we would one day be a normal, happy family. Instead, it was becoming increasingly clear to me that Tommy was not normal, nor did he desire to be anything other than what he was—a selfish, controlling tyrant.

Worse yet, I felt trapped. I hated the person I was becoming and the life my children and I were living, yet I could see no way out. Tommy's threats to kill us loomed over me and echoed through my mind every time I considered leaving.

I'm embarrassed to admit it, but lying became a way of life for me. I covered for Tommy constantly, made excuses for him, and taught the kids to do the same. I didn't discuss Tommy's abusive behavior with our children—maybe because I didn't want to acknowledge it myself, but mostly because we were all busy trying to get life back to "normal" after one of his violent fits. Sadly, they learned at young ages how to manipulate the truth or simply tell "convenient truths"—statements that, while factual, were not actually true. For example: "Dad doesn't feel well today." We all learned it could be dangerous to tell the whole truth, and I hated the lack of integrity in our home.

Granted, on Tommy's good days, we could give the appearance of being a normal, happy family. At times we even had fun together. I watched in wonder as I saw Tommy playing with the kids or teaching them skills. My heart fluttered with joy as I saw them laughing and making good memories together. The kids loved being with their dad when he was happy. At times I witnessed Tommy treating other people with great kindness as well. He'd go out of his way to help someone. People at church loved Tommy and enjoyed his company. He was even nice to me during those occasions.

Seeing these things, I believed Tommy was capable of being a good husband and father. It was also easy for me to convince myself that there was still hope for our family to be okay. But I longed for a home environment where our friends and family members could drop in without me being paranoid that something might slip out about our dark, secret lives.

Of course, we didn't have a lot of visitors at our house, and the kids were seldom permitted to invite overnight guests for parties or sleepovers. Tommy wouldn't allow such things. Tommy had few friends himself, and he kept those he had at a safe distance so they didn't get to know the real Tommy.

We did establish a friendship with a married couple at church with whom he felt comfortable. Our kids were around the same ages, so they played together and had many good times. We even vacationed together, traveling to the Florida Keys so the guys could go fishing and we girls could enjoy the beach and pool. For a few wonderful days, we seemed like a normal family, but I knew better than to share any intimate secrets with our friends.

Normal? Not us.

CHAPTER 17

Missionary Madness

*I*n addition to pastoring a church and developing the neighborhood around it, Tommy's dad was a missionary pilot who flew to Haiti once, and sometimes twice, a week. Tommy had grown up watching his dad fly supplies to missionaries working in Haiti, and occasionally he even accompanied his father—so it wasn't surprising that he had an interest in mission work. What did surprise me was Tommy's unexpected desire to go to Africa to work as a welder, using his mechanical skills to help with the mission's building projects.

We often hosted visiting missionaries at our church, and everyone admired their dedication and enjoyed their fascinating, adventurous stories. Over time we got to know some of the missionaries quite well.

One day, when Tommy seemed more stable, he looked at me and said, "You know, maybe we could make a difference on a mission field." Although his idea seemed far-fetched to some family and friends, it made sense to me. Tommy possessed construction and welding skills, as well as carpentry and mechanical ingenuity.

Also, we had a lot of contacts with missionaries working with needy people in foreign countries.

He initiated a conversation with a missionary organization, and they said, "Yes, we could really use your handyman talents in Tanzania. Why don't you pray about going there?"

Tommy and I did pray about it, as did his parents. We asked the Lord if that was something He wanted us to do.

I felt sure that it would be. I also thought, *Maybe if Tommy feels valued, and maybe if he feels he is doing something that matters, it will change him somehow.*

We applied with World Gospel Mission (WGM), a highly reputable conservative missionary organization headquartered in Marion, Indiana. We traveled to Indiana and spent about a month at WGM's headquarters for interviews and training. While there, we attended class with other couples, and Tommy was the best version of himself. Everyone loved him. He knew how to act and what to say, giving all the right answers to the mission board leaders. He took his medicine faithfully and showed little sign of any chemical imbalance. More importantly, he focused on a goal. When Tommy had something to aim at, he never missed.

Our mentors during training were Dr. Eldred and Louanne Kelley, two outstanding, devout missionary leaders who had attended the same church as my Nana and step-grandfather after they left the Schankweilers' church. They had served with WGM for years and shared so much wisdom with us. They invested long hours in us with such knowledge and love.

Prior to our trip to Indiana, Eldred had shown up unexpectedly at our door in Florida. Louanne was not with him, so I was surprised to see him but welcomed him nonetheless. It was the middle of the day, the kids were in school, and Tommy was working someplace.

"Do you mind if I come in?" Eldred asked unassumingly.

"Absolutely!" I said. "Come on in. What brings you by?"

Eldred was friendly, but he was also quite businesslike. Once we got past the usual small talk, Eldred got straight to the point and asked me a probing question. "Somebody came to me and told me that Tommy has hit you," Eldred said straightforwardly. "I want to get to the bottom of this because it could impact your interview with the mission board."

His question caught me off guard, and I'm sure my face flushed with embarrassment. But I fell back on my default response.

"Oh, no, Mr. Kelley," I lied. "We've had the usual sort of ups and downs as other young married couples..."

"So is there any truth to this?" Eldred asked.

"Well, when we first got married," I said, "yes, he would hit me. But I would hit him too. And sometimes I hit him first. Then he'd hit me back. But that was right after we got married."

"But nothing like that goes on anymore?" he asked.

"No, that was back at the beginning of our marriage," I said. A convenient half-truth.

Eldred liked Tommy and had great respect for Tommy's father. Most likely, he was inclined to give us the benefit of the doubt.

In retrospect, my audacity was appalling. Tommy knew spiritual language well enough to deceive even these strong, discerning spiritual leaders. Part of me felt convicted for lying, for presenting ourselves to others—especially to good, godly leaders—as people we weren't. On the other hand, I was willing to try anything that might help, and Tommy did seem motivated to become a missionary construction worker. If he could become part of something that mattered, something bigger than himself, perhaps he could get his eyes off himself and onto others. And he would feel valued and needed as he helped people who truly could use his assistance. After training, we went before the board; we were accepted and appointed by World Gospel Mission.

The plan was for our entire family to accompany Tommy to Tanzania, with me teaching in a daycare type of setting in Africa. We were genuinely excited about the opportunity.

The downside was that we had to raise our own financial support by going from state to state, church to church, informing the congregations about the ministry and seeking their assistance. The missionary organization trained us for weeks about what life was like on the mission field and what we should expect. This helped equip us with the tools and information we needed to raise funds to finance our new ministry.

Tommy and I met many people along the way who later became dear friends. He was good in front of a group, using humor to deflect his nervousness. He had the ability to make a room filled with people laugh at his stories, jokes, and funny quips. Folks identified with his down-home approach. "I'm just a rough, rednecked boy from Florida," he'd say. "I don't have much of an education, but what I do have is my hands, and I can make things." Then he'd raise his calloused hands to let the audience see he was not afraid of hard work. "I'm a hard worker and can get things done. And the people in Africa have so much less than we do." People seemed naturally attracted to Tommy and wanted to support our family as we prepared to work in Africa.

Although we were having fun fundraising, it was not easy work. We presented the ministry opportunity in churches on Sunday mornings, Sunday evenings, and often on Wednesday evenings as well. In between services, we were on the road traveling to the next location.

At each stop, we told people how we planned to help with WGM's desperately needed building projects in Africa. Tommy talked about the building needs and explained that his skill set was in construction, not preaching. I told how I planned to help with the African children where we would be located, as well as the missionaries' children, while homeschooling our own. Having worked with children in our church and in the daycare, I felt confident that I could do something similar in Africa.

Sometimes we spoke to hundreds of people, and sometimes we shared our goals with just a few folks at a time. Many people we met in the churches were familiar with Tommy's dad and were aware of his reputation for humanitarian work in Haiti. No doubt, they assumed the apple had not fallen far from the tree as they heard Tommy challenge them to help fund projects in Africa. Many people responded positively to our presentations and pledged to support WGM financially.

Despite the new and exciting changes in our lives, and despite spending large amounts of time with solid, spiritual people, Tommy's dysfunction continued unabated behind closed doors. In fact, it seemed to get worse.

To the outside world, Tommy was funny, fun, and full of life. But alone with me, or with our kids in the car, he could be ruthless. Much of our deputation tour took us through Ohio, and with no cell phone or GPS, Tommy got annoyed when we missed a turn on the road or misread our directions. Traversing the winding back roads in a seven-passenger van while trying to follow a map or other directions often proved challenging. Sitting in the passenger seat, and attempting to feed Tommy the next turn, I sometimes missed a road sign. That would irritate Tommy, and he'd reach over and hit me as he drove. It didn't take much to upset him. He was already anxious about the speaking engagement, so any extra pressure ignited his temper.

If his sports coat got wrinkled somehow, or if he misplaced his speaking notes, or if the kids were being too loud as we traveled, Tommy lost it. He'd start yelling and berating all of us. His verbal lashings frequently reduced me to tears by the time we made it to our destination.

One time as we were en route to a church, Tommy got so angry he tore my earring from my ear as we barreled down the highway—all while our children watched wide-eyed from the back seats. Although physically shaken, I knew I had to disguise the pain on the outside. I fought back my tears so I wouldn't have red, swollen eyes when we arrived, but it was hard to transition from Tommy's chaos and cursing to a smiling, happy missionary family.

We must have kept up the façade fairly well, though, because everywhere we went, good people connected with us and supported the WGM ministry. Even though I felt like a hypocrite, I still maintained hope that Tommy would change for the better once we made it to the mission field and he got involved in construction projects. I believed God saw the kids' and my suffering and would make things right for our family one day, so I held on to that glimmer of hope. In the meantime, I prayed for strength to be faithful until God changed our circumstances.

Interestingly, Tommy could put up a good appearance. When we spoke at churches, we presented ourselves as the perfect Christian family. He controlled his temper whenever it was expedient for him, especially in front of a church congregation. But behind closed doors, he made conscious decisions to unleash his anger. How was he going to function in a foreign country, with no accountability other than local missionaries? Still, I was hopeful. I knew Tommy had the potential to do important work using his mechanical skills. I hoped his having a sense of significance and purpose would improve our marriage.

It didn't.

The longer we traveled, the smaller our van seemed to get. We carried a great deal of equipment with us to set up at each church. We had a large film projector and screen, as well as display boards on which we mounted pictures of Africa and typical items used in

Tanzania. All of these things needed to be in place before we met with the congregation.

Because we couldn't afford hotel lodging, we usually stayed with host families from the churches we visited. But as a family of six, that could be stressful as well. We made do as best we could.

We were deeply grateful when Tommy's dad offered to let us borrow his travel trailer. We hitched the trailer to the van and hauled our "home away from home" behind us. When we weren't en route to another location, we parked the travel trailer in Circleville, Ohio, since many of our appointments were in that part of the country. Although the living quarters were tight, we knew it was a temporary situation, so we made it work.

For nearly a year, we traveled together. In each location, Tommy and I presented our intended mission, parading our kids on the platform, all of us smiling as though we were the Brady Bunch. Between the various church services and other meetings, I communicated with the mission offices to coordinate our schedule and set up future appointments. Our schedule was packed, and most of the speaking engagements had to be arranged months in advance, so I constantly juggled travel options. I kept our photo boards updated with current statistics and pictures of Tanzania. I also wrote and sent out newsletters to hundreds of potential donors and spent hours inputting information on my laptop computer after each service.

Since we were traveling out of state, homeschooling seemed the best option for maintaining our children's consistent education. That fell to me as well.

Tommy disliked our tight schedule. "It stresses me out not to have any flexibility," he complained. I understood. He was used to being in control, and during our deputation, he had little over which he could dominate other than the kids and me. He was constantly irritated by the demands put on him by the mission board and the local churches. They directed which churches we would attend, at what time, and for how long. They gave us dates and arrival times for meet-and-greet sessions. Then, after most services, we were to answer questions and meet personally with pastors and potential donors. We frequently met with a group for meals and often didn't get back to our travel trailer until late at night after services.

I enjoyed interacting with the people in the churches where we spoke. To me, it seemed quite reasonable that they would want to get to know us as a family before considering whether to support us financially as part of their missions programs. Meeting the people was an important part of our job, and like any other job, it required commitment.

Tommy groused about every minute we spent on the platform beyond what was absolutely necessary. But he usually did a great job of getting the information out and inspiring people to support the cause. That was especially rewarding to me since I knew the funds we raised went directly to World Gospel Mission, not into our pockets.

One Sunday we had a visit scheduled in one location for the morning church service, followed by another location that night. We made it through the early service without a hitch, but we had no sooner gotten back into the van to leave than Tommy's smile and infectious energy left as well. Once out of the adoring parishioners' sight, Super Friendly Tommy's demeanor turned glum, and he abruptly turned into Mean Tommy, with sharp barbs aimed at the kids and me. It was as if a light switch inside him turned off.

Taking their cues from Tommy, the kids' happy demeanors changed, and they grew sullen as well.

The morning church service had run a bit longer than we had expected, so we needed to hurry to make it to the next one. We'd barely have time to get back to our travel trailer, eat, and freshen up.

Tommy was mad, so he took out his frustration on all of us in the van. I tried to avoid an argument, but nothing I said helped. He grew increasingly irritated and began making awful threats to me. "Just shut up," he said, "or I will drop you at the trailer and go without you."

When we arrived back at the travel trailer, Tommy glared at me and said, "Get out." I picked up baby Tayler and got out of the van. Without opening the door to the trailer, Tommy drove off, taking the three older children with him. I did not have a key to the trailer, and I didn't know anyone nearby, so I sat down on the trailer's front steps. We had no food and nothing to drink. I sat there for hours, swatting bugs and trying to console a crying baby in the dark.

Long after nightfall, around ten thirty p.m., Tommy finally returned with our three older children. I was relieved to see his headlights coming down the road, but he offered no apology. He went straight inside the trailer.

I followed him in, railing at him for his lack of consideration for both me and our baby girl. "You are an awful human being for doing such a thing!" I yelled.

Tommy grabbed a long butcher knife from the counter and raised it to my throat right in front of the kids. "Go ahead." He glowered at me. "I dare you to bring it up again."

Despite Tommy's ups and downs, we recruited new supporters for the mission everywhere we went. We recognized that it would take a lot of money to support our family in Africa, so to stay focused on the goal, I would imagine our family working in Tanzania and making a real difference in people's lives. That vision encouraged me when it was tough and motivated me even more when things were good.

I was still a wife and mother who had to maintain our homelife no matter where we were. The children's homeschooling took up a good bit of my time when we were on the road, but I felt it was the best educational option for them.

For the most part, they seemed to enjoy living in Ohio. They liked the cool weather and had fun playing outside. There was a small patch of woods in the field next to our trailer, and the boys loved to go exploring. Our oldest son, Bubba, loved the outdoors and could spend hours just climbing trees and watching birds or spotting animals. My clothesline hung nearby, so while I was hanging laundry, I let Bubba and Timmy play in the woods.

Tommy often warned the boys that the fields in the woods around our trailer were filled with poison ivy. He showed them the leaves and warned them to stay away from the plants. Bubba, however, seemed to attract the stuff. He and Timmy could play outside all day long and Timmy never got poison ivy. Not so for Bubba. If he even got near it, his body turned red, and he spent the night covered in calamine lotion to soothe the incessant itching.

His dad warned him several more times, but Bubba kept getting into the weeds. Finally Tommy decided to teach his oldest son a lesson he would not soon forget. The next time Bubba came in all itchy from poison ivy, Tommy said, "Stop right there. Take your shirt off."

Bubba obediently complied.

Tommy then proceeded to rub gentian violet, a topical first-aid medication used to treat fungal infections, all over Bubba's arms, face, and neck. I knew what the effects would be and urged Tommy to use calamine lotion instead, but he was insistent upon coating Bubba with the gentian violet. Bubba's white skin slowly turned a deep purple due to the antiseptic dye in the product. Unless washed off immediately, the medication would stain the skin—so Bubba soon looked like a creature out of a bad horror movie. Only his teeth and the whites of his eyes shined through the purple on his face.

"This time he is going to learn," Tommy barked.

Tommy knew the color would fade after a couple of weeks, but he was convinced that by humiliating his oldest son, the boy would learn a lesson. Yet we had deputation duties to fulfill, and he couldn't take Bubba into church looking like the Purple People Eater. Tommy forced him to stay inside the trailer until his skin returned to normal. He no doubt did not want anyone to see the extreme punishment he had inflicted on his son. I hated Tommy for being so cruel and heartless.

For more than a week Bubba stayed inside the trailer with me. The purple faded incrementally, but he still looked awful. One day while Tommy was away and I was hanging clothes, Bubba slipped outside with me. He hadn't been in the sunshine or fresh air for days.

He watched me for a while, then looked up at me and said, "Mom, what someone looks like on the outside doesn't make them who they are on the inside."

"No, Bubba, it doesn't," I replied.

"We shouldn't judge people by the way they look because there's more to them than that," Bubba said. He continued talking about how wrong it was to judge by external appearances.

I realized that Bubba was talking about himself. I nodded in agreement and choked back my tears as I listened. He seemed to be telling me this for his own benefit. At the end of his monologue on fairness and equality, he looked up at me again and said, "Right, Mommy?"

"Yes, Bubba," I said, wiping the tears from my eyes. "You are exactly right." My little nine-year-old son was a hero to me. Rather than being angry about his circumstances, he turned the situation around and found something good in it. Tears flowed down my cheeks as I silently prayed that Bubba would always be able to do that.

CHAPTER 18

Breakdown!

*F*or months our family traveled from town to town, speaking at churches and raising money for our anticipated African missionary work. Tommy's temper flared frequently, and in the close confines of our small travel trailer, there was nowhere to hide. After another vehement argument overheard by our kids, I sought solace in the tiny rear bedroom area and lay down on the bed. It got quiet up front, and I breathed a sigh of relief thinking that Tommy's anger had abated. But Tommy wasn't done. He burst into the bedroom and put a long rifle barrel under my jaw. He spoke slowly and firmly. With a frightening but calm intensity, he said, "Don't you ever embarrass me in front of my children again!"

I dared not move as he kept the gun barrel pressed under my jaw. Fear gripped me and rendered me powerless. It would not be the last time he threatened me with the end of a gun barrel.

We had been on the road for nearly a year and a half, and despite Tommy's often erratic behavior, we were still planning to move to

Africa to serve on the mission field in September 2001. But then in February of that year, Tommy suffered an emotional breakdown during our missionary deputation work in Ohio. Sitting at the kitchen table, he said, "I can't take the stress. It's too much pressure. I just want to die." Tears filled his eyes, and Tommy put his head down on the table, crying convulsively. But his tears no longer influenced me. I had grown numb to them, so I didn't even reply.

Seeing that I remained untouched by his words, he moved to his usual alternative. "Take me to the hospital," he demanded. "I need them to change my medicine. I can't wait until my next appointment. I need to do something now."

This lament, too, had grown stale and meaningless to me, but Tommy insisted that he was having a breakdown, so I drove him to the hospital in Columbus.

The emergency room doctors confirmed that Tommy was having a psychotic breakdown. Shortly after assessing his condition, they admitted him as a patient to the hospital, much to Tommy's chagrin. He wasn't expecting that. He merely wanted more meds. They asked all the usual questions about our lifestyle—about Tommy's habits, about his first bipolar diagnosis, about how long he had been feeling anxious, and about whether he felt he was a danger to his family. Tommy heard those same questions at nearly all of his mental health appointments, so he knew what the docs wanted to hear and how to answer them. But when the doctors asked if he felt he might be tempted to harm himself, he said yes. Oops. Because Tommy admitted his self-destructive feelings, the doctors used the Baker Act to hold him against his will in the hospital. They put him in a mental ward and kept him in a room with rubber on the walls.

This was the second time he had been hospitalized for a mental breakdown. He had spent five days undergoing a battery of tests at Mayo Clinic, where he was diagnosed with depression. Upon learning this, the doctors in Ohio seemed concerned his condition was deteriorating rather than improving.

The doctors asked Tommy, "Do you hurt yourself? Do you hurt your family?"

"No," he lied. Then they asked me similar questions, and I foolishly responded no. Even acknowledging Tommy's irrational actions wouldn't do the kids and me any good unless there was a long-term plan to protect us—which there was not. So there was no point in saying, "Yeah, he beats me every day," or anything like that. Even if they held him in the hospital, he would eventually get out—and when he did, I could only imagine what a nightmare that would be for the kids and me. So I didn't appeal to anyone there to save us.

The doctors, of course, did their best. They had no complete medical history to help them in treating Tommy, so they had to determine their diagnosis based on their observations of him. They concluded that the year of travel away from home and the abrupt career change had taken a toll on his mental health. They added that as someone with a bipolar condition, Tommy should remove as much stress in his life as possible.

I certainly agreed that travel could be stressful, especially with four young children living in a trailer, but I also knew what the doctors did not: namely that no amount of medication improved Tommy's behavior, and no removal of stress would make much of a difference. In truth, he had very little stress in his life already. He simply did not want to continue with the mission work. Beyond that, his inability to do the right thing was totally conditional on his own selfish desires. For instance, when he booked big game hunting trips out of state and away from home for weeks at a time, he had no issues at all. He didn't mind traveling for those trips or even staying with people he didn't know. Why? Because it was something *he* wanted to do.

Also, like so many other things with which Tommy involved himself, once the novelty and the newness wore off, he was done. He was great at pouring himself into something at the beginning, but before long, he got bored or simply stopped trying. He often quit a job and simply walked away without notice or explanation.

But I felt sure he might function differently regarding our commitment to missions in Africa. After all, this was something his family favored and was deeply invested in—emotionally, financially, and spiritually. We had made many public statements proclaiming our excitement about serving people who needed our help. Many people had pledged to support us financially, and several had already given sizable amounts of money to help.

Regardless, mission work was dependent upon relationships with others, something at which Tommy was an abject failure; the task required interacting with people and working as a team. More and more, Tommy realized that he could not control everything in such an environment—and that made him uncomfortable.

This time, however, simply walking away without notice was not an option. But Tommy wanted out, so he had to devise some way to save face with his family and our church folks. In desperation, he manufactured a mental breakdown in which the doctors would prescribe rest. Who could argue with a legitimate health crisis? Poor Tommy. He meant so well; he fully intended to give himself away in service to others.

Yes, he did. For about a year. Now he was ready to go back home, and he intended to get there one way or another.

The doctors kept Tommy in the hospital for a few more days as they reviewed his progress and made some changes to his medications. Then they were ready to release him.

Before the doctors would discharge him, though, he had to sign a form declaring he would have no guns in the home.

Again, I knew he was lying, but I signed the form as well. It was a pipe dream to think that Tommy would rid our home of his multiple weapons. He had an arsenal with guns hidden everywhere in our house, including several in plain sight. But he promised the doctors that he'd remove all of them from our home.

Of course he didn't mean it. He was only telling them what they hoped to hear.

Once we were out the door and in the car, I looked at Tommy and asked, "So what are we going to do with your guns?"

Tommy said, "I'm not getting rid of my guns. I have no intention of getting rid of my guns—ever!"

⁂

We resigned our position with World Gospel Mission and told the leaders we could not carry through on our plans to go to Africa because of Tommy's health conditions. I was terribly disappointed. Of course I had the responsibility—not Tommy—of informing the mission board that we would not be serving in Africa. The money we had raised—and we had raised a bunch, almost enough to finance our journey—would stay with WGM and hopefully fund some other dedicated missionaries and their work.

The days following Tommy's discharge from the hospital were relatively calm, in line with Tommy's pattern after a blowup. He busied himself making calls and preparing arrangements with his family to help us move back home. Although I had certainly missed being so far from family during our deputation, I had enjoyed traveling the country and meeting new people, many of them sincerely dedicated Christians. It was refreshing and encouraging to be around them, to share in their vision to positively affect the world for God.

Tommy always said, "You're a people person, and I am not." He was probably right about that since the only person he truly considered important was himself.

Our family returned home to Florida. Tommy felt defeated, embarrassed, and even more like a failure. Prior to that point, he might get a new job and then stay for nine months or so, but then he'd quit and move on to another job. He rarely returned to a workplace to clean up a mess he had made; he just moved on and broke all ties with his former bosses and fellow employees. But this was worse than losing a job.

When he abandoned the mission work, he couldn't simply break ties and walk away because all the church congregations where we had spoken knew him and his family. Beyond that, his family was involved, and our home church was involved. They had been rooting for us and praying for us to make our goal and enter the mission field. Many of them had contributed money toward our efforts.

So when we canceled our plans, Tommy did not want to return to our home church anymore. "I just don't want to go," he said. When we did venture back to church, he would get mad when well-meaning people asked us after the church service, "What happened? Why didn't you go to the mission field?"

Tommy made excuses to the congregation, but to me, he complained: "It's not their business. They don't need to know any more."

But it *was* their business—especially those people who had prayed for us so faithfully and had supported us financially. They had every right to know why we were not going to carry through with our intended plans.

But Tommy didn't want to hear that. He wanted to distance himself instead.

One day I came home and he said, "We're moving. I don't want to live here. I don't want to be at my dad's church anymore. I don't want to be around these people."

These were people he'd been around most of his life, but suddenly he didn't want to face them.

I made some flimsy excuses to the people at the church, and we moved to Frostproof, Florida—a smaller town in an adjacent county, nestled between Lake Clinch and Reedy Lake. The air moss hung eerily from the limbs of large live oak trees, extending from the tops of the trees all the way to the ground. The area seemed frozen in time. It was not a great distance away from Avon Park, but our home was far enough out in the boonies that Tommy didn't have to see his parents every day or face the people who had supported us in our ministry plans. We lived in a nice yellow house next to an orange grove, and I worked in Lake Wales—a long drive away each morning. For the first time in their lives, our kids attended a public school instead of the private Christian school at Avon Park.

In Frostproof we attended a Baptist church rather than a holiness fellowship, and at first, Tommy liked the anonymity. Before long, however, he slacked off attending. Since he wasn't under his dad's thumb anymore, he only went to church on Sunday mornings. The kids and I continued our practice of going to church every Sunday morning, Sunday evening, and Wednesday night. I especially enjoyed the messages because the emphasis was on the love and grace of God rather than the judgment of God. The kids made friends quickly and got involved in many of the activities of the church—or at least, as many as Tommy would allow. During that time, Tonie Jo committed her life to Jesus.

Getting out of the house and attending church services was a respite for us. At home, the kids and I lived in fear, walking on eggshells all the time, living each day according to Tommy's moods. Timmy, the younger of the boys, was quieter and more timid than his siblings. His dad sensed that and was especially hard on Timmy by intimidating him. Timmy kept his feelings to himself but internalized every strong word or look his dad expressed. He fretted constantly that his dad might be mad at him for some reason. Our oldest son, Bubba, recalls, "When Timmy and I would get off the school bus in Frostproof, Timmy would always say, 'I wonder if Dad's mad. I wonder if Dad's in a bad mood.' The whole way home, he would talk about it and worry whether Dad was in a good mood or bad." It was a nerve-racking way to live.

My relationship with my in-laws and Tommy's sisters remained strong. Tommy's family never acknowledged in any way that they knew something was seriously awry in our marriage, but I think they knew something was wrong in Tommy's life. Since leaving WGM, Tommy worked part-time for his dad as a maintenance man at the church, and increasingly, he butted heads with his own father. Pastor Tom possessed many talents and building skills himself, so he knew what he was talking about. Nevertheless, Tommy challenged him repeatedly, getting into arguments over nothing. Tommy's dad didn't argue. He never lost his temper with Tommy but always answered firmly and reasonably—yet that didn't prevent Tommy from losing his cool.

On one occasion, after another verbal altercation between Tommy and his dad in front of his family, Tommy's older sister came to me and hugged me. As she embraced me, she whispered, "I'm sorry for what you go through." She didn't elaborate, but she added, "I don't know how you put up with it." Tommy's family recognized his temper, and they also knew he could go off on tirades.

But I don't think they knew how bad it really was.

Once we settled in Frostproof, I landed a job at a daycare center in Lake Wales. Tommy found a job as a welder, and although the work sometimes took him out of town, he worked hard and brought home a good paycheck. His supervisors were pleased with his excellent work, but after about nine months, he said, "I can't keep up with the momentum this job requires."

I knew where that was heading. When he got tired of a job, he simply quit. I was no longer even surprised. But as I thought about the future and Tommy's inability to keep a job for long, I knew what I needed to do.

I decided to go back to school and get the nursing degree that I had put off pursuing when Tommy and I married so young. Once married, it wasn't long before Bubba came along, then Timmy, Tonie Jo, and Tayler, postponing my educational plans even further.

I knew nursing school would be difficult, but I was determined to provide financial stability for our family. I recognized that due to our circumstances, juggling home responsibilities along with studies would be challenging.

Still, I was pleasantly surprised when Tommy agreed that I should attend nursing school. I enrolled in South Florida State College and began taking classes to earn my licensed practical nursing (LPN) diploma. Eventually, because of my studies, I had to quit my job at the daycare center—and to replace that much-needed income, I worked with my Aunt Susie in her housecleaning business in Tampa. Aunt Susie taught me the ropes of the professional housecleaning trade, and soon I was able to clean houses closer to my home. The extra income supported our family as I worked my way through nursing school.

I learned to juggle my class responsibilities with being a wife and mother to four children while I cleaned houses at night and on weekends. After class and cleaning houses, I returned home and studied after the kids went to bed. My days were long and

exhausting, but I prayed for God to give me the strength I needed—
and He did.

One of the most encouraging helps I found in keeping my faith
strong was listening to Christian music, particularly the music
associated with Bill and Gloria Gaither and their "Homecoming"
friends, featured in concerts around America and on television.
Years later when people asked me, "How did you make it through
those awful experiences?" I'd often answer, "God and the Gaithers."
I'd listen to the various artists and draw inspiration from the songs.
One song that especially touched me was "Four Days Late" by
Karen Peck and New River. The song dramatically retells the story
of Jesus raising Lazarus from the dead, after His friends had been
upset that He was "late." I was learning that God does not always
do things on our time schedule, but He is never late.

Another artist I listened to on repeat was Nicole C. Mullen,
whose songs "Redeemer" and "Call On Jesus" greatly encouraged
me. It would be years before I discovered that one of the reasons
Nicole's music so resonated with my spirit was because Nicole, too,
had suffered serious abuse by a former spouse.

One day I took Tayler along with me as I was cleaning houses,
and I had Gaither music playing in the car as we returned home. I
was singing along when I looked in the rearview mirror and saw
four-year-old Tayler sitting in the back seat crying.

"What's wrong, Tayler?"

"I just love Jesus so much!" she answered as tiny tears rolled
down her face.

"You do? Well, that's good." I pulled the car off the road by an
orange grove and turned around to look at her. "Baby, do you want
to pray?" I asked her.

"Yes," she said. "I want to pray."

"Do you want to ask Jesus to come into your heart?" I asked her
tenderly.

"Yeah, I do," she responded. I prayed with Tayler right there in the car, that Jesus would come into her heart and she would follow Him all the days of her life. I couldn't help recalling Jesus saying, "Let the little children come unto Me."

While we lived in Frostproof, Bubba developed a friendship with Mason Maxwell, a boy his age and whose family we met at church. Mason lived in the same area as us, and amazingly, Tommy sometimes allowed Bubba to go to Mason's house to ride four-wheelers. It was one of the few friendships Tommy allowed Bubba to have outside of church or school.

A few years later, Mason's mom wrote a letter to Bubba saying, "I knew something wasn't right, but I didn't know what was going on."

CHAPTER 19

Enabling the Disabled

Tommy continued to bounce from job to job, staying at each one only until he disagreed with his employer or his fellow employees. "He wants me to do it this way, but I know it will work better my way," he'd say. Sometimes his obstinacy at work led to heated arguments with his bosses or coworkers—though Tommy never struck one of them as he did me when he got mad. It never took long before he'd quit, and we'd be strapped for money again. We needed his income just to make ends meet, so I tried to encourage him to find a new job as quickly as possible. Fortunately, he was a talented and skilled worker when he wanted to be, so he did not remain unemployed for long.

Most of his frequent and sudden job changes could be attributed to his inability to effectively communicate with others or to maintain relationships. Although he did little to preserve any of his friendships, he usually made some small efforts to get along with his coworkers. But after a while, I noticed he was less interested in even doing that much. The charm he once used to impress other people seemed too much effort for him now. More and more, he tried less and less. It seemed he was increasingly disconnecting from everyone.

I struggled to eliminate as much stress from his life as I could, as his doctor had recommended. But much of his stress was the direct result of poor judgment on his part. For instance, he often bought high-ticket items we didn't need, things our tight budget couldn't support. Then, when we couldn't pay our bills, he'd get mad.

When he had a confrontation or disagreement with his mom, dad, or any other family member, rather than trying to resolve the issue, he simply avoided the person involved. Not only would he stay away from his family, but he also barred the kids and me from visiting them or having anything to do with them. If I tried to inter-vene, Tommy vented his anger in my direction.

In the same way, he'd get angry at his coworkers if he didn't get his way. He'd throw a tantrum and threaten to quit. That added more pressure on me, of course, because I was already carrying a heavy load with school, work, and caring for the kids. I worried how we would survive without Tommy's income, but he simply didn't care.

So it frustrated but didn't surprise me when I learned he had walked off another job while I was in nursing school. He blathered on about why he couldn't work there, but taking responsibility for his own actions was a foreign concept to Tommy. It was always somebody else's fault. Everyone else was wrong and he was right. Trying to convince him otherwise was futile.

Tommy complained about the stress at work so often and so vehemently, his doctors eventually advised him to seek disability status. They said stress exacerbated his bipolar disorder. That's all Tommy needed to hear.

Applying for disability—which would result in his receiving compensation from the government based on his inability to earn a living—became Tommy's total focus. That meant acquiring disability status for Tommy shot to the top of my priority list as well, whether I wanted it to or not. I was the person who had to track down all his job information, fill out all the forms, and procure the medical records from the various doctors Tommy had seen over the years. Tommy did nothing to help. Nothing except to yell about how long it was taking me to complete the application. No question, it was a tedious and time-consuming process, with a nebulous goal of Tommy not having to work. We sought help from the Mayo Clinic because one doctor after another had declared Tommy as bipolar. Tommy was declared unable to work because of his physical and emotional disability; the doctors said he was manic-depressive.

Once I completed the stack of paperwork and submitted Tommy's myriad doctors' reports, his case was reviewed. It was a joyous day when we received word in return that Tommy was eligible for disability income.

The disability check he received each month was not near the amount he could earn as a welder, but a welder had to actually go to work, do the job, and maintain a decent relationship with the employer and fellow employees. Tommy didn't want to do that. He took the government check instead.

Being declared disabled simply made matters worse, giving Tommy another valid medical excuse for behaving so badly. He latched onto that and played it for all he could get out of it. At times he blamed his abusive behavior on missing his medications. On other occasions he didn't even bother trying to transfer blame or explain his belligerence. He simply railed, "What do you expect from someone who is bipolar? This is just who I am."

His apologies grew fewer and less sincere, while his excuses increased commensurately.

While I was thankful we had some reliable source of monthly income, our budget was now tighter than ever. Perhaps worse yet, Tommy now had time on his hands. He had nowhere to go. Nothing to do.

Maybe that's why I was surprised one day when Tommy said, "I think I want to go back to school."

I knew better than to discount the idea or to raise the obvious objection: "How are you going to pay for that?" Instead, I feigned interest and asked, "Oh, really? What would you like to study?"

"I want to become a surgical technician," he said without a moment's hesitation.

"Really? That's interesting. Are you serious?" I asked. Thanks to both Nana's and my mom's backgrounds in nursing as well as my own nursing school education, I knew surgical technicians worked right in the operating rooms with surgeons, preparing and keeping the surgical instruments in the hospital at the ready. This was not a low-stress environment.

Besides working as a corrections officer, Tommy had only worked in construction, landscaping, and welding. He had never expressed interest in surgery before. Whatever made him think he might want to work in that field? Maybe he thought he could reinvent himself through a new career. I had no idea, but I was intrigued.

I assumed Tommy's new fascination with becoming a surgical technician would soon pass. He was always coming up with new ideas of some project he wanted to do. But we didn't have the money. I guessed that this phase would soon fade as well.

But it didn't. In fact, Tommy spent a great deal of time researching information about how he might get started. He found a private school in Tampa that would give him a student loan so he could start taking classes immediately. He worked out a plan with my mom in which he could live with her in Tampa while he was in school, rather than making the trip back and forth to Frostproof every day.

Mom loved Tommy, and except for the orange juice incident that had taken place nearly a dozen years earlier (which she had attributed to Tommy's travel stress), she had never seen the person the kids and I saw at home. She was delighted to have Tommy stay with her during his classes.

Tommy traveled to Tampa on Sunday nights, and then came home late on Friday afternoons. In truth, I didn't mind Tommy being away from home for a week at a time. His absence made life easier for the kids and me; we didn't feel as though we were constantly walking on eggshells in our efforts to avoid riling his temper.

The kids never mentioned the domestic violence in our home to their teachers at school. On only one occasion were the school authorities put on alert, and ironically, they were concerned about *me* abusing our kids! While I was in nursing school and Tommy was in Tampa, our youngest daughter, Tayler, had done something mischievous with her siblings, and when I asked her about it, she lied to me. I wasn't upset, mean to her, or out of control in any way, but I wasn't going to let her get away with that sort of behavior either.

"Well, you need to get one swat for lying," I told her. I reached for my thin belt with one hand and grabbed her arm with the other. She wriggled out of my grasp and took off running away from me, crying. I ran after her and brought her back inside.

"I'm sorry, Mommy," she said.

"Okay, I forgive you," I said, "but you are still going to get a swat for lying."

I took the thin belt and gave her one swat on her bare legs. I didn't hit her hard, but the end of the belt wrapped around her leg and left a welt. I immediately placed her in the bathtub and put something cold on her leg. I felt horrible that the belt had left a mark.

The next day, little Tayler marched into her kindergarten class, pulled up her skirt, and showed her teacher the red mark on her leg. "Look what my mommy did to me," she told her teacher.

The teacher reported the incident, and Children's Services came to our home to do a full investigation of *me*. They asked all sorts of questions, including to the other siblings, such as, "Has your mom ever hit you?" The older kids all responded in the negative, and none of the children mentioned anything about the violence in our home caused by their dad.

ᴏᴔᴓ

Tommy liked his studies to become a surgical technician and made good grades, and not surprisingly, his teachers liked him. He made several new friends there, and the timing of the classes greatly facilitated him getting along fairly well with my mom. Mom worked night shift at the hospital, and my brother, Billy, who lived with Mom, worked during the day while Tommy was in school. So they all spent little time together in the same room, which worked to Tommy's advantage.

Tommy studied hard and completed the program in fifteen months. He became a certified surgical technician and was hired at a hospital in Sebring.

Do I need to tell you what happened?

In less than two weeks, Tommy quit his surgical technician job. "It's too high a level of stress," he complained.

I had tried to warn Tommy about the tension in an operating room. Surgeries are often life-and-death situations with no room for error. Preparing the wrong surgical instrument could be deadly.

But as usual, Tommy did not listen to my advice and brushed off my opinion that the role of surgical technician might not be for him.

I wanted to say, "I told you so," but I knew better. Besides, what good would it do? We were on the line for a high-interest loan for Tommy's new career—and once again, he was unemployed.

CHAPTER 20

Tennessee on My Mind

While Tommy was in Tampa for fifteen months, I finished my own medical studies to become an LPN. Tommy seemed proud of me, and I knew he was relieved that we could count on my steady income. After my graduation, Highlands Regional Hospital in Sebring offered me a position on the medical/surgical floor, and I was delighted to accept. I had completed much of my clinical work at Sebring, so I knew the routines and had already established relationships with many of the nurses and doctors. Going to work there as a new nurse on the team was exciting to me. I made new friends and felt good about myself.

My schedule was busy but fulfilling and working on the surgical floor was challenging and exciting. I began my shift at the hospital at seven a.m., so I had to be clocked in by six forty-five a.m. to receive the overnight reports from the night nurse. I got up early each morning to have some time alone before the kids got ready for school. I had established a habit of rising early to have some time with God, to read the Bible and pray, and to listen for His voice at the beginning of each day. I vigorously protected this time because

I knew I needed the strength I received from God even more than I needed sleep.

My days were filled with one crisis after another, caring for patients going into surgical situations or coming out of them. It was stressful and draining work, but I loved the satisfaction I felt in helping others. I ended my shifts physically and emotionally exhausted. Most days I didn't get home till eight p.m.

As I drove home each evening, I fretted over what circumstances awaited me. I knew the kids got off the school bus around four p.m. and Tommy would be waiting for them, not necessarily with a happy greeting. Tommy always expected them to work with him on his latest projects as soon as they arrived home. While most of their classmates went home to play or do their homework, my kids were coerced into doing whatever chores and projects Tommy had in mind. Some of these were adult-sized projects far beyond their years or skill sets, but Tommy wanted them done quickly and correctly. He had no patience or tolerance for mistakes, especially from Bubba or Timmy.

With nothing but time on his hands, Tommy became restless. He spent long hours on a computer exploring ideas for projects he wanted to pursue or some new invention percolating in his brain. But after numerous dead ends, he found other areas of interest on which he focused his attention: namely, real estate. We had been living in Frostproof for nearly three years and he was itching to move again, so he began searching online for properties for sale in states other than Florida.

When he mentioned his property searches to me, I responded less than enthusiastically. Why would we want to move again? We were settled nicely in our new community. The kids were happy at school and had made some new friends. I loved my job as a nurse, and our church was only a short distance down the road from our house.

But similar to most decisions regarding our family, Tommy didn't ask how the kids or I felt about such matters. On his kinder days, he merely pretended to be interested in our opinions. He even enlisted my help in his computer searches for property during my days off work.

He had his own rationale for moving. "Moving to a different state would give us a fresh start," he said. He didn't elaborate on what that meant.

Tommy became enamored with moving to Tennessee. Although I didn't understand it at the time, I later realized he wanted to move us far from his family and church members who knew him well. I had mixed feelings about another move—especially all the way to Tennessee. I loved Florida and didn't want to leave again, but I hoped that perhaps a new location, far away from the recent embarrassments of our missions failures, might help reduce Tommy's stress levels and give us some breathing room.

Knowing that I was still skeptical of his plan, Tommy began lobbying the kids. He knew they were my weakness, and if he could convince the kids that moving was in their best interests, I'd soon cave when it came to any opposition. He was a master manipulator who treated all of us like puppets.

While browsing online, Tommy discovered several potential properties in rural Tennessee that had plenty of room for the kids' pets. "Moving there would change our lives and really make a difference in my mood swings," he told the kids and me. I had to admit, the houses Tommy found did look interesting. The properties included acres of woods and sparkling streams that would provide good hunting and fishing. The properties seemed to offer the country lifestyle of seclusion that Tommy talked about so often. He knew, of course, that I preferred living closer to stores, schools, hospitals, and churches, but my desires were irrelevant to him. Mile by mile, he had slowly moved us farther and farther away from family and community, making his control over us absolute. "It would be nice to live in a place where I don't have to answer to my family for a change," he huffed.

That attitude scared me. Although I never ran to Tommy's parents for help, it was reassuring to know they were nearby—just in case.

Moving to another state became Tommy's new passion. While I hoped he'd lose interest after looking into prices, he only grew more fascinated with the idea of moving. He asked me to make some phone calls and talk to Realtors—something I was loathe to do. "It gives me anxiety to talk to the real estate people," he told me, knowing I would do almost anything to keep him from becoming stressed to the point of another outburst.

Over time, Tommy convinced the kids that we'd be better off in Tennessee. He told Tonie Jo she could get a horse, and he promised the boys they could have minibikes and four-wheelers to bounce over the fields. Tayler was still young enough to be excited about the occasional snow that covered the landscape during Tennessee winters, albeit briefly. Tommy campaigned incessantly about the benefits of moving, and the pressure built commensurately.

I allowed myself to dream a bit. What if it were true? What if the slower pace of country living would help Tommy function better? Could we really have a "normal" life? Slowly, I grew willing to risk it, believing we had little to lose and everything to gain. I agreed to move. "But not until the kids finish out their school year in Florida," I told Tommy.

"It will probably take a while for our house here to sell anyhow," he said, "so that should work just fine."

We put our home in Frostproof on the market, and much to Tommy's surprise and my chagrin, we received a cash offer from a buyer almost instantly. We hadn't even found a place in Tennessee yet, but we'd have to accept or reject the offer soon. We decided to take a whirlwind trip to Tennessee to explore some of the properties we had seen online.

Late one night after I had worked a full shift at the hospital, our family headed toward Tennessee. Since I had just completed three twelve-hour days in a row, I had four days off before I was scheduled to return to work. We planned to drive to Tennessee, spend a day or two looking at potential real estate deals, and then drive back in time for me to get to work.

The kids slept while Tommy and I drove through the night. The next morning, we met with Realtors and viewed various properties. None seemed attractive to us. Later that day, we met with another agent who showed us other properties.

Prior to our trip, we had found online a small two-bedroom country home with twenty-two acres of property in Lawrenceburg, Tennessee, about a ninety-minute drive from Nashville. The second Realtor arranged for us to view it. "It's just a short ride out the way there," he said with a heavy drawl.

As we headed out of town, I noticed cornfields lining the miles of winding two-lane highway, with rolling hills off in the distance. An occasional house dotted the landscape with not much else in between. I was slightly nervous about being so isolated, but then we passed an elementary school. That eased my mind a bit. We couldn't be too far out if a school was nearby. We traveled on for several more miles and I spotted a peaceful, old-fashioned-looking church, complete with a steeple. The sign in front of the church read: Deerfield Baptist Church. God has never spoken to me audibly, but that day, I heard the words in my spirit: "That's your new church."

We continued driving until we came to a long driveway where I saw the house I recognized from the online photos. It was a modest-looking redbrick house that sat back off the road. It was only a two-bedroom home, but it had an unfinished basement that

Tommy felt he could turn into bedrooms for the boys. That made sense to me, since Tommy was not working and needed a project. The property looked beautiful even to a city girl like me. There were plenty of wooded areas for hunting and two ponds for fishing, one of which could be seen from the back porch of the house. Tommy and the kids seemed excited, so I was hopeful.

After touring the house and the property, we were convinced. The price was right, and Tommy especially liked the large amount of acreage, replete with rolling hills and thick green woods. I cancelled our other real estate appointments. We were sold.

Back in Florida, we signed the papers to sell our house and set the wheels in motion for the life-changing move to Lawrenceburg, Tennessee. We scheduled our move during the 2005 Thanksgiving break.

Tonie Jo turned eleven years of age right before our moving day, so we invited our family to help us celebrate her birthday. It was a bittersweet time, especially for my mom. I knew she would miss seeing her grandchildren and me after having us nearby. The hour-and-a-half drive between Tampa and Frostproof seemed inconsequential compared to the twelve-hour drive separating us once we moved to Tennessee. I was going to miss my mom terribly—again!

We loaded all of our possessions into a large Penske rental truck and headed north on the interstate, traveling the length of Florida, through Georgia, and into southern Tennessee. The kids seemed happy as we set out on this new adventure. I wasn't happy about leaving Florida, but for the sake of the others, I pretended to be thrilled. I was anything but thrilled.

Still, I couldn't deny that an almost palpable difference pervaded the atmosphere as we got closer to our new home. The kids were excited to experience the change of seasons, and Tommy seemed to be having fun with them as we traveled. Just watching and listening to our family laughing and talking about all the things they wanted to do together lifted my spirits. Maybe this move would make a difference. Maybe our nightmares were behind us.

After many long hours in the truck, we finally pulled onto Piney Road, the lane leading to our new home. We were thirteen miles away from the nearest Walmart, though there was a small family-owned convenience store, Self's Market, near our lane. The kids were fascinated with the house since it had a staircase leading downstairs to the basement. Our homes in Florida did not have basements, so that was an attractive feature, especially to the boys.

We took our time unloading and unpacking. I had purposely not sought out a new job yet but planned to do so after the holidays, in hopes of taking the time we needed to get our new home set up first.

Following a bit of rest, Tommy wasted no time getting started on the basement remodeling project since the house had only two bedrooms on the main floor—one for Tommy and me, and the other for Tonie Jo and Tayler. We set up temporary sleeping areas in the basement for the boys until we completed the remodeling. The basement was a large, spacious area with a woodstove in the center. Tommy and I made frequent trips to the local hardware store. Inevitably, as I was checking out at one of the stores in Lawrenceburg, someone would ask, "Oh, are you the new family that just moved here from Florida?"

"Ah, yeah, that's us," I'd say.

"Well, welcome! We're so glad y'all are here."

I soon learned that nearly everyone in town knew each other. Nevertheless, I was still surprised when a few days after moving in I heard a sharp knock at our back door. It was winter and already dark and cold outside, but when I opened the door, I saw a friendly woman whose face beamed at me with a big smile. She introduced herself as Gail Dixon, our neighbor who lived on a farm down the road. She had brought us some homemade treats as a welcome gift. When Gail learned that Tommy was working on a remodeling project in the basement, she told her husband, Bill, and he came over to help the next day. Without hesitation, Bill jumped right in to lend a hand, as though he and Tommy were old friends. To Bill and Gail, "Southern hospitality" was more than a mere slogan. The friendly people in our new community made us feel right at home.

We celebrated our first Tennessee Christmas, and life was busy but good. The kids quickly acclimated to their new schools, and I found a nursing job in Lawrenceburg. And sure enough, we found a ready welcome at Deerfield Baptist Church. Church attendance remained part of the kids' and my lives, but Tommy rarely went along with us. Nevertheless, the kids met new friends at church and became involved in some of the activities—as Tommy permitted. For me, the church was a place where I could relax physically—a peaceful atmosphere where I could refresh and maintain my spiritual stamina. My faith in God sustained me, and I met several new friends at the church who would have a profound influence in my life in the days ahead.

As I'd done in Florida, I worked several twelve-hour days so I could have more days at home but still earn the same amount of money. Tommy busied himself with the basement remodeling project. I was cautiously optimistic that the move to Tennessee would be life-changing after all. I could not have imagined how life-changing our relocation would be.

⚬⚬⚬

We had been living in our new home for about three months when my cousin Britni contacted me and said she would like to visit.

Britni and her sister, Brandi, were my two closest cousins on Mom's side of the family. About ten years younger than me, they seemed to enjoy hanging out with me, and I had always liked picking them up in Tampa and taking them shopping or to the movies. They often spent the night at our house, and later, when I had kids of my own, Britni and Brandi loved to host my kids overnight too.

Tommy rarely allowed our kids to stay overnight at anyone's home, but for some reason, he liked Britni and Brandi and got along well with them. He didn't mind our kids staying with them occasionally.

Britni had been working in Illinois as a nanny. That job had ended, but she didn't want to return to Tampa; she was interested in what Tennessee had to offer. Tommy was open to helping her, and we offered to let her stay with us. I was delighted because the kids loved her, and I knew she would be a helper since I was working such long hours. Like many of the women in my family, she had an interest in the medical field, so I felt confident I could help her find a job in the area. Tommy had seemed more content since the move, so I was hopeful that he would not have any conflicts with my younger cousin.

Britni moved in with us in January 2006. Our family enjoyed having Britni, and even Tommy seemed pleased. She was a great help around the house, and I helped her get a nursing assistant job at the rehabilitation center nearby. She soon established herself as a valued coworker and made many new friends.

Since she was an attractive twenty-five-year-old woman with a lot going for her, it was not surprising when the young men in the area took notice of Britni. She dated several nice guys, going on hiking and fishing trips, motorcycle rides, and other activities, and she never gave me any reason to be concerned. Soon, however, Tommy took more interest in who she was dating and what she was doing. He even introduced her to one of the guys with whom she went out. All seemed fine until his controlling nature flared.

Tommy set a curfew for Britni and demanded she be in at a certain time. Moreover, he imposed his opinions on who he wanted her to date. As an adult woman, gainfully employed and her own boss, Britni balked at Tommy's overbearing attitude.

"That's totally unreasonable," I told Tommy when he demanded Britni avoid a certain fellow.

Tommy responded angrily. "Nobody tells me how to run my house!" he yelled. Then he pressured me to have Britni stop dating completely. "You'd better control your cousin," he told me.

But there was no reason for his concern. And I told him so. "It's not your place to police Britni's life," I said, "even if she were doing something wrong—which she isn't."

"She's living under our roof," he roared, "so she'd better straighten up."

His demands grew increasingly ridiculous. One night when Britni was out past Tommy's arbitrary curfew, he locked her out of the house.

Tommy must have realized that he did not have a strong hold over Britni, so as he often did when he couldn't control a situation or people in his life, he lashed out physically in some other way. The next time Britni's date came to the house to pick her up, Tommy wouldn't allow him in the driveway, so Britni walked to the main road to meet him instead. Meanwhile, Tommy grabbed a rifle, stormed down the stairs, and went out to the back driveway. He furiously fired into the concrete wall alongside the driveway, sending shards of fragmented cement in every direction. Tommy had used this tactic on me previously, and it had worked since I was worried the kids might get hit with a stray bullet or cement fragments. Plus I knew I'd have to work harder to earn enough money to repair the bullet-ridden driveway.

But Britni did not have those concerns. After Tommy shot up the driveway, she decided it was time to leave permanently. Tommy immediately went into damage control mode. The next day, Tommy told me, "Ask Britni if she wants to go with us to buy some Easter bunnies for the girls." I passed along the message, and Britni accompanied us.

But she also called her parents and made arrangements for them to come get her. About a week later, they came and helped her move out.

As he had many times, Tommy apologized profusely to me and made up some excuse for his erratic actions—he tried to be nice, hoping he could smooth things over with Britni, but she wasn't buying it.

While waiting for her parents to arrive, we were sitting in my car. In private, she asked me, "Are you afraid of him?"

I stared out the car window for the longest time.

"Why don't you leave with me?" she asked.

"I want to more than anything," I told her. "But I can't." I didn't say any more. I knew that if my family members ever challenged Tommy about his temper, he would not back down—so I did not want to get them involved. "I love him," I told Britni.

It wasn't true. I'd stopped loving Tommy long ago, but it was too complicated to explain. I recognized that Tommy's dangerous temper was getting harder to hide and was slowly leaking out for others to witness.

Britni nodded. She didn't understand that my fear of leaving outweighed my fear of staying.

CHAPTER 21

Moonshine Madness

O ne downside of the move to the Volunteer State was that Tommy discovered Tennessee moonshine: homemade whiskey produced nearby. Although Tommy had not previously imbibed, he soon became addicted to the alcohol, drinking large amounts of inexpensive whiskey nearly every day. The alcohol, especially when mixed with his psychotropic medications, worsened his moodiness and erratic behavior.

Before this time, I had only witnessed Tommy drink an occasional beer. His family, of course, had deep convictions against drinking alcohol, so as far as I knew, Tommy had complied with his parents' wishes to abstain. But now he was drinking hard liquor, and a lot of it. His habit began slowly, then quickly escalated to a bottle of whiskey every week. Before long, he was drinking at least one bottle of Evan Williams bourbon every three days.

Besides being inebriated in front of our kids, Tommy's drinking also took a toll on our tight budget. He'd buy alcohol before he'd purchase food for the family. No matter how many times I tried to caution him, "Tommy, we can't afford this," he'd buy another bottle, usually two, so he wouldn't run out between my paychecks. He smelled of liquor constantly.

His rages got totally out of control. His voice grew louder, the arguments longer, and his outbursts and fights more brutal. I begged him for mercy during these episodes. He turned into a different person, rampaging and roaring through the house until he eventually passed out in an intoxicated stupor. The kids and I resigned ourselves to the mess because we could not go on with life until we had cleaned up the broken glass, swept up any debris, and covered the holes in the walls where Tommy had punched his fists through the plasterboard.

Tommy no longer apologized for his behavior after he began drinking and mixing his medications. In fact, when I told him the next day what had happened, he often refused to believe that he had done the horrible things he had done. "You're just making that story up to make me look bad," he said.

One time he drank so much that he vomited all over himself and passed out in the middle of the kitchen. Bubba, Timmy, and I had to drag Tommy into the bathroom, strip off his flannel shirt and coveralls, and get him into the bathtub. It was gross, and I felt ashamed that our teenage boys saw their dad that way.

The next day, when I tried to tell Tommy how awful it had been for the boys and me, he railed, "You're lying! You're just trying to manipulate me so I won't drink." He refused to accept the truth or take any responsibility for his actions.

Over the next two years, the rage became much worse as he turned into an alcoholic.

Away from the watchful eyes of his family, Tommy did not even try to maintain appearances any longer. He ate terribly, putting on dozens of pounds, and let his hair grow long and scraggly. Instead of dressing neatly, he often resorted to sloppy coveralls and a t-shirt. He looked more like a member of Hells Angels than a holiness preacher's son. Maybe that's why I wasn't surprised when Tommy splurged on a brand-new Harley-Davidson motorcycle.

CHAPTER 22

Do We Really Need a Harley?

Our finances were tight even when Tommy was gainfully employed. But with the six of us living on my income and his disability check, making the money stretch far enough to cover our basic monthly bills was a constant battle. We always seemed to have too much *month* at the end of our money. I worked out one budget after another in attempts to live within our means. Tommy acquiesced for a while and allowed me to pay the bills, but then just about the time I could cover our living costs, Tommy started a new project or decided he needed a new toy.

"My mind is constantly in motion," Tommy told me. "It never seems to slow down or shut off. I can't sleep at night because my brain is still working on a new invention."

I understood and knew Tommy was not exaggerating. He had a brilliantly creative and innovative mind when it came to mechanical things or construction ideas. He probably could have been a successful industrial engineer if he had ever put his mind to it. He sketched out ideas for new inventions or projects all the time, and once he locked in on something, he became obsessed with making it happen, regardless of the cost.

Because of his impulsive nature, Tommy lacked discipline to follow through on his plans. Once he got an idea, he wanted to see it come to life quickly, and usually got bored if it took too much time or effort. Rather than ruminate on a project and save the money to finance it, Tommy simply robbed the money he needed from our small nest egg or bill-paying account. It didn't matter to him if we were behind on our monthly bills, so long as he had enough money to pay for what he wanted. That's why our budget never worked; Tommy was always busting it for no good reason. We were constantly in debt or behind on payments, with exceedingly high late fees tacked onto our ever-mounting bills.

Tommy often spent our monthly income before we even received it. His disability check was a fixed amount, but my income fluctuated with the amount of overtime I was able to work. I cautioned Tommy again and again that we had little discretionary income and couldn't afford anything but necessities for a while. But he was home day after day with time on his hands, so he found numerous ways to keep us in financial debt. If he wanted something, he simply bought it, whether it was for a speculative project he had dreamed up overnight, or new parts for his truck, or building supplies for something he wanted to invent. Whether we could afford it was irrelevant to Tommy. He wanted it and was determined to get it.

I stressed to him that we should prioritize expenses such as the mortgage, groceries, and the electric bill, not to mention keeping my car on the road, with the insurance paid and gasoline in the tank. I needed a dependable car to make the thirty-mile commute to work every day.

Tommy didn't care. To him, every one of his inventions could be the next big thing. Unfortunately, none were.

On one occasion, knowing that every penny was budgeted and that we did not have any wiggle room for extravagances, Tommy took his entire disability check, drove to Nashville, and made a hefty down payment on a brand-new Harley-Davidson motorcycle. Worse yet, he locked us into monthly payments that we absolutely could not afford. I had been working that day, and when I returned home that evening following a long, tiring shift there was the Harley sitting in front of our house.

I was irate, but I was also exhausted, so I didn't want to argue. I knew that by confronting Tommy, I was asking for another beating I wasn't sure I could take. Nevertheless, I had been working twelve-hour shifts, four days a week to provide for our family, while Tommy spent money on his liquor and toys faster than I could bring it in. So I wasn't about to ignore his nonsense. I broached the subject to Tommy. "How can you do this?" I asked. "We can barely make ends meet now. What did you think you were doing? Why did you buy a motorcycle?"

Tommy responded violently as I dared to object to his foolishness. He hollered at me, and I hollered right back at him.

"You know we are behind on our mortgage payments," I said, "and I've been working hard to get us caught up again."

Tommy didn't want to hear the truth, especially when he knew he was wrong. He yelled louder and chased me around the house, trying to grab me by the hair as he usually did during our arguments, but I eluded his grasp. He lunged at me again and missed.

Somehow, when Tommy turned his back to me, I made it out the front door, dashed off the porch, and dove behind a row of hedges at the end of the driveway. I was barefoot and breathing heavily from the chase. Tommy knew I was hiding somewhere, but maybe because of the liquor in his system, or because he assumed he could simply wait me out, he didn't step off the porch. Nor did he see or hear me panting behind the hedges.

He went back inside, then returned to the front porch after a few minutes and just stood there. He had my flip phone in his hand and held it up above his head, perhaps assuming I was watching. I cringed when I saw him snap the phone in two and throw it into the yard. He then walked over to my car, lifted the hood, and unplugged some wires so I could not escape.

Satisfied that he had slowed me down sufficiently, he went back inside and slammed the door.

I stayed outside in the bushes for hours. I was hot and thirsty but determined to remain hidden until it was safe to go back in the house. Eventually Tommy fell asleep. He was unable to beat me physically that day, but his foolish purchase beat down my spirit.

CHAPTER 23

Canned Tomato Terror

As a boy, Tommy learned from his mother how to can fruits and vegetables, and he enjoyed preserving his tomatoes in glass Mason jars. He stored an entire assortment of canned vegetables in our kitchen cupboards. One night when he lost his temper again, he began grabbing his own workmanship, whipping the jars of tomatoes to the floor, and shattering the glass. Tomatoes and juice splattered in every direction. One or two jars of canned tomatoes would have made a mess, but Tommy continued his unhinged rant until he had destroyed more than twenty jars of canned tomatoes he had so meticulously worked to preserve.

The kids were terrified by the noise, but also by the realization: *If Dad would do that to something he worked so hard to preserve, what would he do to us?*

Tommy's rampage went on into the night. At one point the kids and I watched as he ripped the stove away from the wall and then single-handedly heaved it outside. He seemed to possess supernatural demonic strength during these times, and no ordinary man or woman was a match for him.

That same night, Tommy grabbed me by the neck and literally lifted me off the ground, his tight grip clenched around my throat. I tried to wriggle away from him but couldn't. Soon I felt my consciousness fleeing away from me.

Just then, Bubba ran into the room with a rifle in his hands. "Put Mom down!" he yelled at Tommy.

I could feel Tommy's grip around my neck grow even tighter. He glared at Bubba, and a hint of a devious smile pierced his lips. He released his grip on my neck, and I collapsed to the ground. Tommy walked straight toward his teenage son without a bit of hesitation. He shoved his finger into Bubba's chest and said, "Boy, if you ever point another gun at me, you'd better make sure it is loaded. Now get outta my house!"

Bubba looked at me on the floor, then back at his dad. He didn't argue. He put the gun down and left. I later learned that he spent the night out in a field, sleeping next to a bale of hay near some cows.

Meanwhile, I stumbled to my feet and hustled Timmy, Tonie Jo, and Tayler downstairs where they could hide from Tommy. I found one of Tommy's many guns and held it tightly in my hand, with my back against the wall. I slid down into a corner of the room, my eyes peeled for any sign of Tommy coming down the steps. I shooed the kids into the unfinished rooms downstairs and stood guard. He'd have to get through me first if he wanted to get to them. I nervously tightened my grip on the gun in my hands. I hoped I had loaded it correctly. I had no idea.

There was no carpet on the basement floor, and I sat on the cold cement for what seemed like an hour. I could hear Tommy, still on a rampage upstairs, breaking up more of our house. All the while he kept yelling, "Sandee Jo! Get up here! Get back up here right now."

I didn't budge. If he wanted me, he'd have to come after me—and I'd be ready for him. I was ready for the madness to end.

Tommy continued yelling my name from upstairs, but I was too terrified to answer him. I expected him to come roaring down the steps at any moment and was surprised he hadn't yet done so. He almost always pursued me when he wanted to fight.

He yelled my name again and again as I sat on the floor, cold and shaking. "Come on upstairs, Sandee Jo," he said in a more subdued voice. "I won't hurt you. Promise." Then he added, "I'm really sorry for getting so upset. Sorry I scared the kids too." A few more minutes went by before he said, "I need your help, Sandee Jo. I'm bleeding." His voice sounded eerily calm, and he seemed sincere.

I finally took a chance and ascended the steps. When I saw the mess in the kitchen, I could hardly believe my eyes.

Tommy wasn't satisfied. He wanted the kids to come up as well. He made them line up and then sit down on the kitchen floor, in the middle of the smashed tomatoes and broken glass. "I have something I want the kids to hear," he announced loudly, looking at me.

He turned to face the kids on the floor and said, "I want you to listen to every word very closely."

I had no idea what he planned to do. This was usually the time for his apology speech—telling us how sorry he was, how badly he felt about his behavior, and begging us for forgiveness. But his twisted thinking took another wild, warped turn that night. While he did tell the kids he was sorry, he quickly included a disclaimer: "But what happened here tonight was not my fault." He forced me to stand in front of him and the kids as he ranted about what a terrible wife and mother I was. "If your mom hadn't made me so angry"—he waved his hand at the mess on the floor—"none of this would have happened. If your mom were a better wife to me, I would not act this way and lose my temper." He forced me to grovel before him, demanding that I apologize to him. Then he dropped his pants and forced me to kiss his butt cheek in a demeaning, indecent manner, right in front of our children.

That night I could not imagine his dehumanizing and humiliating behavior getting any worse—yet at the same time, I feared it might.

CHAPTER 24

Good Dad; Demonic Dad

As odd as it might seem, when Tommy was in his right mind, he was a fun dad to the kids. For instance, we realized early on that it would be helpful to have a four-wheeler to traverse our property in Tennessee. In Florida, the most land we ever had was three acres. Now we had twenty-two acres of rolling hills and wooded land where a four-wheeler made much more sense than trying to access it by car or truck. Tommy found a good buy on a four-wheeler and bought it for the kids to ride. They took turns buzzing up and down the green hills on the four-wheeler, and Tommy often joined in the fun. He played around with the kids, went fishing in the ponds on our property with them, and sometimes went hunting with them in the woods. He'd laugh and act goofy with them, just like a normal dad might do. They loved being with him in such moments. I lived for these days, and so did the kids.

Since the boys monopolized the four-wheeler, Tommy started looking for a horse, as he had promised Tonie Jo when we were first discussing a possible move to Tennessee. Now that we were residents of the area, we learned quickly that horses were common in Davy Crockett country, and there were always plenty of beautiful horses for sale—some for really good prices. We found advertisements announcing "Horse for Sale" almost everywhere we went. Pictures of available horses were posted in the grocery stores, on telephone poles, and on the Internet as well.

When Tommy found a beautiful horse named Annie for only five hundred dollars, we couldn't pass up the bargain. He hooked up a trailer to his truck, and we went to pick her up. After meeting the owner and talking about Annie for a while, we loaded her into the trailer and took her home.

Tonie Jo was ecstatic. She had wanted a horse for so long, from the time she had first watched the movie *Pocahontas*, and now she had one of her very own. Tommy helped Tonie Jo get accustomed to a real horse, teaching her how to feed, brush, and care for Annie. Each day after school, Tonie Jo headed down to the barn to spend time with Annie. She couldn't do much riding yet. Annie was a big horse and quite spirited, still needing some training to get used to a saddle on her back. But Tonie Jo didn't mind. She patiently loved Annie at her best and at her worst.

The man from whom we had purchased Annie had tried to warn us that Annie wasn't highly disciplined and seemed to have a mind of her own. That didn't bother us. Any animal lover knows that even the best and most tame animals can sometimes be unpredictable, and Annie certainly fit that bill. She didn't buck or bite, but she did love to break out of the fence around the pasture. Annie broke through the fence several times. Each time Tommy repaired the fence, he reinforced it to prevent further escapes, but Annie was a smart horse and—like a magician—found the weak spot in the fence and disappeared into thin air.

Regardless of Annie's bad habits, Tonie Jo adored her. Tommy, however, was not so patient or forgiving. He threatened to give the horse away if Annie would not stay within the pasture fences. I knew that would break Tonie Jo's heart, so I begged him to give Annie a little more time. Meanwhile, I prayed the horse would behave!

She didn't.

On a day I had off from work, I was trying to catch up on things around the house when I received a phone call from a neighbor. They had found Annie wandering around a field, several miles away from our home. I sighed sadly at the news. "I'm so sorry," I said. "But thank you for letting us know. We'll be right there to get her."

Tommy was furious when I told him Annie had escaped the fence again. Never having a deep well from which to draw anyhow, his patience was exhausted. He and I went to retrieve the horse from our neighbor, put her into the trailer, and drive back to the barn. Tommy spewed vitriol toward Annie all the way there and back. We had no sooner gotten Annie back inside the barn before Tommy turned to me and snarled, "I'm gonna put a bullet in Annie's head."

I gasped. "No, Tommy!"

He acted as though he didn't even hear me and was talking with himself. "She's never going to be worth anything," he growled. "All she's doing is costing us money."

I had seen Tommy like this before, and I knew what usually came next. Occasionally I could talk Tommy out of reacting violently to a situation, but at other times, my pleadings only spurred on his impudence. It all depended on his mood. I quietly suggested, "Why don't we take Annie back to her former owner?"

Tommy nixed my idea. "No, that won't work. That's why she was so cheap. They didn't want her either." A sick feeling gripped my stomach as I stared at the massive creature with her dark, beautiful eyes.

Tommy had already made up his mind. He took off toward the house, on a mission. I trailed behind him, struggling to keep up.

"Let's advertise her in the paper," I said. "We can say, 'Free horse to a good home,'" I suggested.

Tommy only shook his head as he stormed into the house. He had guns hidden in every room, and several in plain sight. Some were in a gun cabinet, one was in a closet, a couple more were propped up against the wall next to our bed, and another one was stashed by our kitchen window. He kept a gun beside his recliner and two more hidden above the ceiling tile.

I knew once Tommy had a weapon in his hand, it would be harder to talk him out of his impulse. He wasted no time and went straight to the firearm he wanted, shoving bullets into the chamber and yelling at me at the same time. "There's already a big hole down by the wood line," he said, "right where the creek runs. I've been planning to go down there and burn some trash, so we'll take the horse to that spot, and when I shoot her, she will fall into the hole. I'll start a fire and burn her with all that trash. Then I'll cover up the carcass with dirt."

I was so stunned by his devious plan that I didn't utter a word. I simply stood there in shock as he kept feeding ammunition into his gun. Finally, he looked up at me and told me my role in this tragedy. "You have to hold her by the bridle so I don't miss," he said matter-of-factly.

With his gun still in hand, he took off downstairs. "Hurry up!" he said. "I want to be done before Tonie Jo gets home from school."

He gathered shovels and a full gasoline can and strode off toward the barn. I ran behind him, hoping I could yet change his mind. I didn't even want to think about the pain Tonie Jo might experience at the destruction of her horse, but I knew what Tommy was capable of when it came to killing the kids' pets.

When I first met Tommy, he showed me a picture of himself with a cute little dog. Tommy looked to be about fourteen or fifteen in the photograph. "That dog was the best pet I ever had," Tommy had told me. "She was my hunting buddy, and we used to spend long hours together in the woods. That dog was the closest thing I ever had to a best friend. I trained her and taught her tricks. She was so faithful to me. But that all ended the day I accidentally ran over her with the truck."

I had heard Tommy tell that story on numerous occasions. It always ended with him tragically running over his beloved dog.

Then one day, Tommy told me the truth. He had gotten extremely angry over something unrelated to his dog, took the dog out to the woods, and shot her.

At the time, I could not believe anyone could be so heartless and cruel. How could anyone kill a defenseless animal like that? But in the years since that time, I had learned all too well how someone could do such a thing. I had witnessed the horror of it with my own eyes as Tommy killed one of our family pets after another, usually in some cruel and violent manner.

Still, Annie was more than a pet gerbil or even a pet pig. This was a horse—a large, full-grown horse!

We arrived at the hole near the creek Tommy had described. He grabbed a shovel and dug around the edges of the hole, making it larger. When it was the size he wanted, he went back to the barn to get Annie. I walked beside Annie on her unwitting death march to her grave. I hoped against hope that Tommy might change his mind at the last minute, or that the horse might spook, break free, and run away. But none of that happened.

"Stand right there," Tommy ordered me. "And hold the bridle like this."

My hands trembled and Tommy noticed. Surely he knew I did not want to be a part of this grossly inhumane act, but he didn't seem to care.

I begged Tommy one last time. "Please, Tommy, please don't hurt the horse." He seemed unfazed, so I tried a different tact.

"Tonie Jo will hate you for this," I warned. But nothing I could say deterred Tommy from his plan. The horse would not obey him, so the horse was going to die.

I kept begging, and finally Tommy became so exasperated with me that I thought he might shoot me *and* the horse. "Just shut up and go back to the house," he finally relented.

I covered my ears tightly with my hands and headed back toward home, expecting to hear the blast of the gun before I made it inside. Once inside, I kept my hands over my ears; I didn't want to know when Tommy shot Annie.

I didn't hear the shot, but soon Tommy returned to the house. He looked spent himself. "That was really hard to do," he said. "I wish there could have been another way."

I looked back at him blankly, as though to say, *Are you kidding? There were plenty of other ways. You just didn't want to do any of them.* But I said nothing. I was too upset to talk about it.

"Don't tell Tonie Jo," Tommy warned. He had already devised an entire fictional story with elements of fact that he planned to tell our daughter. "We'll start out with the truth," he said, "that the horse got through the fence again." He nodded, seemingly pleased with himself for telling the truth. "We drove to get her, and I led her back home as you followed behind in the car," he said. That was still basically true.

But then Tommy said, "A guy with a horse trailer stopped and commented on what a nice-looking horse Annie is. I offered him a deal on her, and he took me up on it." To Tommy, this was a compromise. Tonie Jo would still be devastated that we had sold her horse, but she wouldn't know the horrible truth.

I put my hands over my face to hide my tears. I hated Tommy and hated myself for covering up for him.

CHAPTER 25

Kill Me!

*I*ncreasingly, Tommy's violence toward our children was volitional; his lashing out at them was not spontaneous or accidental. It was willful and expressed on purpose. Once Tommy took apart a ceiling fan and kept one of the flat, wide blades. "This is good," he said, fondling the fan blade in his hands. "I can spank them with this, and it won't leave a mark." Clearly he was thinking through his plans to punish the boys—but not for any wrongdoing. He rarely disciplined the kids as corrective action. To Tommy, discipline and punishment were one and the same.

He often beat the boys by whipping off his belt and hitting them with the buckle end of the strap, leaving large welts on their bodies.

Tommy spanked the girls almost as much as the boys. They'd retreat to their bedrooms, whimpering and sobbing. Tommy never tried to console them after a spanking or talk with them about what they had done wrong. Never did he say, "This hurts me even more than it hurts you." He'd spank them and they'd cry, and he'd simply move on with life as normal.

Despite Tommy's cruelty, when the kids were younger, we prayed as a family each night. We would kneel down by their beds before bedtime. I can't imagine how confused their spiritual understanding must have been.

Our family's existence continued to be colored by Tommy's drinking, which grew even more pronounced after we had been in Tennessee for a while. Worse yet, Tommy began forcing his liquor on Bubba as well. One night we were sitting out by a campfire on our property enjoying a peaceful evening, but then Tommy began drinking and didn't stop. After a while, he wanted Bubba to drink with him. Bubba was only sixteen years old, but his dad kept saying, "Here, drink, kid. Some more. Drink some more."

Tommy handed Bubba one straight shot of Evan Williams after another. "Take a swig of this," Tommy pressured him. In a desperate attempt to keep his dad from getting mad, Bubba drank and drank and drank. "Take another sip," Tommy said, laughing. Finally poor Bubba got so drunk he couldn't even walk. As we made our way back up to the house, Bubba fell over. Tommy started yelling and kicking him in the ribs. "Get up!" he yelled at Bubba as he lay curled on the ground. "Stop acting like your mother!" Tommy kicked him hard again.

"Dad, I'm trying!" Bubba cried. He pushed his dad away from him.

"Don't you ever put your hands on me again," Tommy spat, and he and Bubba tussled in a drunken stupor.

"Leave him alone!" I yelled at Tommy. I reached down and tried to help Bubba regain his footing. He tried to stand up and take a step or two, but he slumped to the ground again. It took a while, but Bubba finally made it up to the house.

I struggled to get everyone into bed while Tommy passed out drunk in our bedroom. Afterward, weary and fatigued, I fell asleep, too.

The next morning, I awakened Bubba and asked, "How are you feeling?"

He roused from the intense hangover and mumbled, "I don't know, Mom. I don't even remember coming back up to the house from the fire last night. I didn't want to drink that stuff, but I didn't want to make Dad mad either."

"I know, Bubba," I said. "I'm sorry."

Tommy began unleashing his venomous attacks on Bubba as much as me. It got to the place where Bubba couldn't do anything to please his father, no matter how hard he tried. That become clear when Bubba got a job with our neighbor to earn a bit of spending money.

Drunk, and angry that Bubba was working after school at the neighbor's farm rather than coming directly home to help him, Tommy repeatedly threatened to kill our oldest son. From the kitchen I could hear him cleaning his rifle on the back porch, shouting, and yelling out my name intermittently. I tried to ignore him, hoping his anger would subside. But he grew louder, insisting on my attention. Tommy then came inside and found me in the kitchen. "How dare that boy do that!" Tommy roared at me, expressing his anger that Bubba had taken the job. "Did you know about this?" He pushed his face up in front of mine, and the sickening smell of sour booze wafted toward me. I didn't answer.

"Who does he think he is?" Tommy continued to rant. "We work *here* first. He works with *me* first!"

I thought of trying to calm him, but in his inebriated condition, there would be no reasoning with Tommy.

He shouted, "I'll shoot him when he gets home. You watch!" He stomped back to the porch and busied himself with cleaning his gun. "I'll shoot him," he said again. "I'll teach him a lesson!" he yelled repeatedly, with increasing volume and intensity.

Like so many other times I was sick with fear, but I was also disgusted. I'd had enough of Tommy's nonsense. Finally I walked outside and shouted back at him, "Stop talking that way! You are being totally irrational." I should have stopped there, but I didn't.

"If you're determined to kill someone today," I yelled in his face, "kill me! I'm tired of your games, and I'm sick of these constant threats."

I knew my words were useless. Tommy had already had too much whiskey. He yelled louder and louder, so I walked to the bedroom, hoping to put some space between us. Along the way I grabbed one of Tommy's long-barreled .22 caliber rifles, which he kept loaded and propped up in the corner of the room. I didn't even know how hold the gun, much less how to aim or fire it, so I held the weapon awkwardly by the barrel. For some reason, I thought having it in my grasp was a good idea.

Wrong!

The next thing I knew, Tommy burst into the bedroom. He saw me with the gun, and we started to struggle over it. He grabbed the rifle and began waving it at me, as he shouted right in my face. I held the cold gun barrel with all my might and tried to turn it away from me, but as we struggled, I tripped and fell backward onto the bed. We continued wrestling on the bed as I fought hard to keep the barrel away from my face. But Tommy was too strong for me. The long part of the gun barrel wedged against my head, pressed against me, and I felt the strong vibration and the deafening explosion as it went off.

In the struggle, apparently, I had jerked my body just far enough at the last moment—so the bullet missed my head and lodged into the shelf behind me. I had some knickknacks on the shelf along with Tayler's baby photo album. The bullet pierced the album and exited the other side.

I lay crying on the bed as Tommy took the gun and shoved its barrel all the way through the drywall of our bedroom, until only the gun's stock was sticking out. But Tommy wasn't done yet. He took our dresser and heaved it through our bedroom window, shattering the glass all over the floor. I curled up in a fetal position, frozen in fear, as he wreaked havoc throughout our bedroom, destroying anything I treasured or considered meaningful, shouting loudly at me the whole time.

I don't know if he intended to kill me that day or just scare me. But I got the message.

CHAPTER 26

The Phone Call Out of the Blue

About three weeks before Easter 2008, Tommy received a totally unexpected telephone call from James Crocker, a high school friend from Hobe Sound, the private Christian school Tommy had attended. I was enrolled in college again and working toward my registered nursing degree, so I was sitting on the couch with my lap covered in books when the phone rang. Tommy was sitting in a recliner nearby when he answered the phone and discovered it was his old friend James. I didn't really know James, but at some point after our wedding, I learned that James Crocker had been one of the two groomsmen who had "kidnapped" me until the wedding guests coughed up enough cash to pay my ransom. Innumerable times since then, I had wished the guests had been too stingy rather than too kind.

Tommy talked to James for a long time, which surprised me. It was not like him to take a call from a friend; he had alienated himself from anyone who knew him previously. Sitting in the same room, I could overhear parts of the conversation. James invited Tommy to attend their class reunion, but Tommy refused. "I got hair down the middle of my back, I'm tattooed from head to toe,

I'm a hundred pounds overweight, and I haven't worked in three years," Tommy told his former classmate. "Trust me. Nobody from that school would want to see me." He declined James's invitation.

That didn't surprise me. Tommy *had* gained a lot of weight since our move to Tennessee. He was depressed and disconnected from most of his former friends and even family relationships. In rebellion against his dad's conservative views, he had covered his body with tattoos. He felt he had nothing to live for. I heard him tell James that he wasn't physically or mentally happy, and that his life hadn't turned out how he had hoped.

When he hung up, Tommy told me that James had invented a machine and built quite a successful business. He looked at me and said, "That's the kind of guy you should have married—someone who did something with his life instead of a loser like me."

My deep well of compassion for Tommy had long since run dry. I knew he was simply trying to evoke sympathy from me, wanting me to feel sorry for him, so I would attempt to cheer him up.

I was over it. I ignored his comment.

Sandee Jo. (2024)

Sandee Jo with brother Billy and Mom in her Nurse's uniform. (1977)

Nana, Sandee Jo, and Mom—my two greatest influences growing up. (1987)

Tommy and Sandee Jo's wedding day. A week later Tommy shoved me for the first time. (1989)

Sandee Jo and newborn Bubba
(black eye almost healed).

Family of Four —Sandee
Jo holding Timmy, Tommy
holding Bubba. (1993)

Family of Four—Tommy
holding Timmy
and Sandee Jo with
Bubba. (1993)

Family of five—Mother's
Day 1995, the day the
A/C broke in our car
and Tommy erupted.

Family of five—
Tommy's beloved
cowboy hat that I
pitched in the fire the
day I called 911. (1995)

Family of six—
Sandee Jo holding
baby Tayler. (1998)

The
Schankweiler
Family

Serving
in
Tanzania, Africa

Tommy   Tonie Jo   Sandee Jo   Tayler   Tom   Timmy

Family missionary photo. We sincerely hoped to help
others, but we needed help even more. (1999)

Easter 2000.

Annie (the horse Tommy shot) and cousins Brandi and
Britni with Tayler and Tonie Jo. (2005)

One of our last family photos, Christmas 2007.

TOP: Pickax with which Tommy threatened to "split Bubba's head like a melon," and a piece of cinder block thrown at Bubba. (2008)

BOTTOM: Wood thrown at Bubba and cinder block wall chipped away by Tommy, Good Friday 2008.

TOP: 2×4's Tommy hurled at Bubba, Good Friday 2008.

BOTTOM: The shovel, another of Tommy's weapons used against Bubba that fateful day.

TOP: Work area where Bubba cut the wrong board and made his dad angry.

RIGHT: The basement door that Bubba slammed when running from his dad and the glass shattered, later boarded up by Timmy.

The boarded-up bedroom window after the fight when Tommy discharged his gun near Sandee Jo's head.

James announcing the Gatlinburg vacation to the family.

TOP: Family leaving for the mountains in a limo.

BOTTOM: Project Tent for food and shade. More than
130 volunteers helped renovate our home.

TOP: Construction in process.

BOTTOM: Saturday evening home reveal. So many friends to cheer us on!

Buttermilk, move that tractor!

Pap and Granny at Project Fresh Start. They remained
dedicated to our family even after they lost their son.

Kitchen/Before.

Kitchen/After.

Pap pinning Bubba at military
graduation. (2011)

James and Sandee Jo's wedding day
with Tayler and Charlee. (2015)

James and Sandee Jo in Prague. (2017)

CHAPTER 27

A Dark Good Friday

D o you remember the old jokes that started out, "You know it's going to be a bad day when…?" Such as: "You know it's going to be a bad day when your waterbed breaks, but then you remember you *don't have a waterbed!*" Or: "You know it's going to be a bad day when your six-year-old boy says, 'Mom, did you know that it's *almost* impossible to flush a grapefruit down the toilet?'" Yep, that's going to be a bad day.

For me, I knew it was going to be a bad day when I heard Tommy's derisive laughter emanating from the basement shortly after nine o'clock in the morning. That meant he had already started drinking heavily on what was supposed to be one of the most holy days of the entire Christian calendar—Good Friday, the day on which Jesus was crucified.

It was March 21, 2008, and Tommy and I had been married for more than eighteen years. I should have known better than to agitate him when he was drinking. I should have just stayed away from him.

But I didn't.

Instead, like walking right into a hornets' nest, I headed downstairs to the basement to do a load of laundry that morning. That's when I saw my husband outside the basement entryway working on his motorcycle. I also noticed that he was working on a new bottle of Evan Williams. By this point in our marriage, Tommy was a full-blown alcoholic, although he would never admit to that. After all, he was a preacher's son, and preachers' kids don't become alcoholics.

Or do they?

Tommy bought moonshine and other less expensive booze by the half-gallon jug, and he normally drank through one or two of those each week.

Sometimes, if I asked Tommy nicely, and if he was in the right mood, he would curb his drinking for a couple of days. At other times, he became irritated if I even mentioned it. I always knew I was taking a chance when I approached him about his alcohol consumption.

On that morning, as I loaded the clothes into the washing machine, he walked through the basement door to tell me something. I could smell the whiskey on his breath, and the sour odor sickened me.

It's barely nine thirty in the morning, I fumed to myself. Still, I kept my disgust concealed behind an expressionless face. To have any chance of appealing to him about his drinking, my words needed to be laced with kindness and gentleness. Any other approach could ignite his explosive temper. Like a seething volcano, he was perpetually ready to erupt from just one poke, prod, or misplaced word by me.

So I put a strained smile on my face and presented a pleasant demeanor. "Tommy, can you just be really careful and please keep a handle on how much you are drinking today?" I asked, knowing I was taking a chance. "It's Easter weekend," I reminded him, "and I'm off today because of Good Friday, but I'll be at work the rest of the weekend. The kids are looking forward to an extended weekend out of school. Maybe you can do something special with them while I am at work tomorrow and Sunday."

Before I could finish my plea, he snapped. "You'd better watch how you speak to me. Don't you tell me what I can or cannot do in my own house. Who do you think you are, criticizing me for drinking?"

I recognized that tone of voice. I could tell I had crossed the line, so I tried to diffuse the tension. "I'm your wife, Tommy, and the kids love you. They want to spend Easter weekend with you."

I sensed that he would hold this against me for hours, maybe all day long. He never let things go easily. As he walked away, he yelled to our two teenaged boys, "Bubba, Timmy, meet me outside. Now."

I turned away from him and went back upstairs. I said a quick prayer under my breath and then sat down on the couch to read. I knew I had irritated Tommy, and now the entire household would suffer as a result. That was his pattern.

With Easter upon us, I had already decorated the kids' Easter baskets. After stuffing them full of chocolate candies, jelly beans, marshmallow Peeps, and other goodies, I had hidden them away in our bedroom closet so our curious, snoopy children couldn't get into them until Sunday morning. My work as a nurse at a local rehabilitation center would keep me away from home almost the entire weekend. I would miss Easter Sunday, one of my favorite celebrations, the resurrection of Jesus from the dead. Tommy had stopped attending church by now, and I had no illusions that he would take the kids to church service. So I had prepared everything ahead of time so the kids could at least enjoy discovering the treats in their baskets, even though I wouldn't be there to share in the fun with them.

Our thirteen-year-old daughter, Tonie Jo, was at a friend's house, and our two barely dressed boys had gone outside to help their dad. I sat at the end of the sofa reading to our nine-year-old daughter, Tayler, from a children's Bible about this special holiday. The book detailed the events leading up to the crucifixion of Christ in such a simple and meaningful manner that even a child could understand. Tayler sat quietly and contentedly, relaxing beside me, listening as I read.

Suddenly, a loud noise jolted Tayler and me out of our sweet reverie. I recognized it immediately as the sound of shattering glass. This was an all-too-familiar noise within the walls of our home, but never one I got used to hearing.

I had hoped for a peaceful, spiritual weekend. But now this. You know it's going to be a bad day when…Only this was no joke.

⚬⚭⚬

As soon as I heard the shattering glass, my heart sank. I guessed that Tommy had lost his temper with one of the boys. I wasn't wrong. Our oldest son, Bubba, came running up the stairs from the basement wearing only blue jeans. Without saying a word, he ran through the living room and out the front door to the yard.

"Stay inside the house," I told Tayler, her eyes now wide with anxiety. I jumped up from the couch and bolted outside as well.

Although Bubba was tall and physically fit, I knew he was no match for his father when he was angry. My husband's vitriol and violence usually came on without warning, resulting in what seemed like supernatural strength surging through him. The only safe response was to steer clear of him.

I hollered to Bubba, "Run, Bubba! Run away!" At that point I had no idea what was going on, or if he was being chased by his dad. Nor did I have a clue why his father was angry with him. The whys were irrelevant. They didn't really matter once Tommy lost his temper. The only thing the rest of the family members could do was to get out of harm's way.

I later learned that as Tommy and our two boys had been doing some carpentry work on the back patio area, Tommy continued to drink from a bottle of Evan Williams. When seventeen-year-old Bubba made a minor mistake in cutting a two-by-four, Tommy erupted, yelling about the waste of lumber and threatening his son. Tommy picked up a large metal framing square and hurled it right at Bubba's head. Had the boy not ducked quickly, it would have sliced right into his face or worse. Had the square hit Bubba's neck, it could have severely injured him. Bubba fended off the dangerous tool with a stainless steel pan, and when he saw the large dent it left behind, he knew he didn't stand a chance. He threw the pan at his dad and ran for the door. Our fifteen-year-old son, Timmy, had witnessed the entire incident. As Bubba ran back into the basement in his attempt to elude his dad's anger, he had slammed the door so hard the window shattered. That just made matters worse.

Unfortunately, this sort of irrational incident was no longer unusual in our family—but that didn't mean it wasn't scary. It was. It always was. Tommy's unrestrained outbursts frightened our children and me nearly to death.

Bubba had barely gotten out the front door when his dad came roaring up the basement stairs. Wearing lace-up boots, jeans, and a flannel jacket, Tommy lumbered through the living room, ripped open the front door, and stormed out into the yard, just seconds behind our son.

Seeing Tommy chasing our Bubba, I knew time was not on my side. I needed to put myself somewhere in the middle, in between father and son. I ran behind my husband, got close, and clutched his flannel jacket, trying to slow him down. I pushed him and grabbed at him in a desperate attempt to make him fall. It was obvious that he was drunk, so I knew his equilibrium was off. If I could just cause him to lose his balance, I might be able to keep him on the ground long enough for Bubba to escape.

But Tommy had far more strength than I had. He turned in my direction and shoved me so hard that I fell backward. I recovered my balance and lunged toward him again, evoking more violent responses from Tommy. He repeatedly swung his fists at me. Because of his inebriated condition, he missed me—a lot—which made him even angrier. When he did connect a blow to my chest, it sent me reeling. My body seared in pain, but I couldn't afford to wallow or whine. I knew I had to keep Tommy distracted, if only for a few precious seconds, to give Bubba a chance to put more distance between him and his dad. I continued struggling with Tommy as long as I could before he flicked me off him like a dog kicking off a flea.

I rolled onto the ground and bounced to my knees, watching Tommy to make sure he wasn't coming after me. I had one thing in my favor: I knew I could outrun him. I had always run faster than Tommy, and my long legs had saved my life on several occasions. In truth, I wished he would come after me rather than Bubba—but I wasn't the focal point that day. For some reason I did not yet know, Tommy was intent on catching our son. I knew it wasn't so he could tell him how proud he was of him, or how much he loved him. Quite the opposite. For more than a year, along with me, our firstborn son had increasingly become the object of his dad's wrath—the frequent recipient of Tommy's verbal and physical abuse.

Bubba fled around the front of the house to the backyard, with his dad chasing closely behind him. The tools they had been using on the construction project were sitting right where they had been abruptly abandoned when the fracas had begun. Tommy grabbed several hand tools and hurled them at Bubba. With the agility of a young deer, Bubba sidestepped the tool flying toward his head, then another aimed at his midsection.

When he missed his target, Tommy bellowed in anger. Chest heaving, he took a moment's break, gulped some air, then resumed the chase. Bubba continued to run.

I hurried to keep up with them. "Tommy, what's wrong?" I yelled to my husband. "Why are you so mad? Please, let's talk."

Fat chance of that. He didn't answer. I knew there would be no discussion until he had gotten what he wanted—and apparently he wanted to hurt Bubba.

Every attempt I made to de-escalate the out-of-control situation failed. I realized my only hope was to keep them separated until Tommy was exhausted. Each time my husband stopped to catch his breath, I pleaded with him, "Tommy! Please! Stop! This is crazy!"

He ignored my cries and resumed the chase.

Tommy's loud bellows and my screams seemed to reverberate off the trees surrounding our property. We lived out in the country with a lot of space between houses, so I didn't anticipate any of our neighbors hearing the commotion and coming to help Bubba and me. We were on our own trying to fend off a madman.

At one point, Bubba stopped running, turned, and faced his father from a distance. He cried out sadly, "Dad! Why are you doing this?" The chase stopped for a moment and became a standoff. Tommy bent over, huffing and puffing, then raised his head and looked back up the yard toward Bubba. Tommy glared at our son ferociously.

Tommy's response was a guttural roar, followed by hurling bricks, broken pieces of cinder blocks, and a hammer in Bubba's direction. Tommy threw with such incredible precision and force; it was obvious that he was not merely trying to scare or bruise his boy. He wanted to kill him. This was not the first time Tommy had threatened to kill his son or our other children. Bubba seemed to sense that it would not be the last.

The mayhem continued unabated. It went on for more than an hour, then another hour.

From a safe distance, Bubba again plaintively called to his father, begging him to think about what he was doing. "Dad, please stop! Why are you doing this, Dad?"

There was no explanation and no excuse for my husband's belligerent behavior. Our best hope was that he would run out of steam, fall down, or better yet, pass out from alcohol-induced drowsiness. Until then, attempting to reason with him was futile.

"Just run, Bubba! Get away from here for a while," I yelled to him.

At that point, I was not particular about where Bubba should go. I simply wanted him to hide someplace safe and out of the destructive path of his father.

But I knew my son, and Bubba didn't run from trouble—especially if he suspected the rest of us were in danger. Moreover, Bubba knew the awful truth about running, just as I did. I had learned the hard way that staying in the grips of a violent fight with Tommy was dangerous, but that fleeing from it could be much more painful. Tommy hated when I ran from him, and when I did, the consequences were devastating if he caught me. He'd push, shove, and slap me, drag me around by my long hair, and choke me to within a whisper's edge of death.

By age seventeen, Bubba also knew the routine of these fiery rages. He had been on the receiving end of many of his dad's volatile outbursts.

But he had also figured out his dad's behavior patterns. We both knew Tommy's fury usually ascended to a pinnacle, his disgusting and profane threats reaching an earsplitting crescendo, but then he would eventually crumble like an avalanche. When the earth stopped shaking, he ordinarily turned into an eerily calm version of himself. Calm Tommy was sad, remorseful, and regretful, willing to say or do whatever it took to redeem himself. The tears soon followed, and Tommy became weak emotionally and physically. In those moments, he seemed so sincere that he convinced us he would never—ever—behave so badly again.

Following this scenario, I could expect at least a couple of days of peace as Tommy lived out his remorse by being exceptionally kind and helpful to the family. During those times, he was actually a good dad, playing with the kids and teaching them how to do creative and fun things they wanted to do. But all too soon, Calm Tommy disappeared and Tyrant Tommy returned.

No doubt, as Bubba kept a safe distance between himself and his dad, he was trying to outlast his father. He was hoping his dad would become exhausted, give up the fight, and collapse like all the other times. Bubba was a faithful son who loved his father and wanted his abusive ways to end. He was a good kid who didn't have a vindictive bone in his body. He had never attempted any sort of retaliation or retribution against his father during or after his rampages.

But something about this situation seemed even more extreme than usual. I had often felt afraid during Tommy's erratic and violent outbursts, but everything about this rampage felt different. I felt more than fear; I had a sense of impending doom, a feeling that this day was not going to end well, that it was like no other day our family had ever experienced.

Meanwhile, Tommy found a pickax among the scattered tools and swung it as he shouted ominously at Bubba, "Do you see this?" He brandished the pickax above his head, then slammed it against a board lying nearby, splintering it. "I'm going to split your head like a melon!" Terrified, Bubba ran for his life—literally—with his drunken father chasing after him, lurching along in a drunken stupor, wielding the pickax, screaming profanities, and repeatedly threatening his life.

His words made me physically sick, the revulsion churning my stomach. This was not a joke; it wasn't a horror movie or a video game. Tommy's words were not idle rants. I felt certain that somebody was going to die, either Tommy or me. I was not about to let Tommy carry out his threats against our son. I would not let that happen. I couldn't. I was determined that the ax would go through me before it ever hit my son.

I screamed for Bubba to keep going. "Just run, Bubba!" I cried. "Don't stop. Don't turn around. Just run!"

CHAPTER 28

God, Where Are You?

The chaos continued well into the afternoon. With his face beet red and a robotic look in his eyes, Tommy's lunacy was on full display as he hollered out in detail all the ways he planned to kill Bubba. When I caught up to Tommy again, I took a full swing at him and tried to shove him down, to no avail. He simply brushed me off, my body scraping roughly across the ground. I scampered to my feet, keeping my eyes on the pickax Tommy still held. I knew that at any point, he might hurl the ax toward me—he'd done similar things before—or he might simply chop at my arms or legs or head. He was so out of his mind with anger and alcohol, there was no telling what he might do.

I ran ahead, trying to position myself between them every chance I could. Occasionally, when Tommy caught up to me or I caught up to him, I grabbed him and wrapped my arms tightly around his waist or legs in a desperate attempt to slow him down. But he pushed me down to the ground each time. At one point I found the belt loops of his blue jeans and pulled with all my might. I thought surely I could get him to the ground by yanking on his belt, but his belt loops ripped instead. No matter what I did, I failed. I was no match for him as he dominated the situation with his brute force and seemingly otherworldly power.

Staying near him, I continued to interfere with every attempt he made to resume the chase. Every time I slowed him down, he got even angrier. He swung hard at me, but I was able to dodge most of his blows. After he shoved me down near the area where the boys had been working, I spotted an iron crowbar on the ground. As I stumbled back to my feet, I picked up the crowbar and hid it behind my back.

I stealthily moved up closer to Tommy, planning to hit him in the head with the crowbar and hopefully knock him to the ground. I was terrified but running on adrenaline. I knew Tommy's strength better than anyone and realized I had only one chance to bring him down with the iron bar. If I missed, it would be all over. If I failed to knock him out with one blow, Tommy would turn in an instant and use the tool on me. And he would not just hit me once.

I quietly crept up behind Tommy, grasping the crowbar in my hand. But just then, I made eye contact with Bubba, who was standing across the yard in the grass, catching his breath. He saw the crowbar and slowly shook his head as if cautioning me, begging me not to do it. He well understood the consequences of such a risky counterattack.

I stared at the back of Tommy's head. I was only a few feet away—all I had to do was swing the bar hard—but then I looked back at Bubba. I felt the strength drain from my arms. My limbs drooped, and I dropped the heavy iron crowbar at my feet. I had never before felt so helpless and weak.

Tears welled in my eyes as I looked up to the sky and cried out. "Where are You, God?" I yelled. "Why aren't You helping us? We need You!"

I was mere seconds from collapsing. By now, the altercation had been going on for a couple of hours. I was physically and emotionally spent. My body was bruised and battered and limp from trying to prevent Tommy from hurting our son. I couldn't take any more.

Suddenly the clouds in the sky appeared to be swirling above me, as if I was looking up at them while riding a merry-go-round. Then everything moved as if in slow motion, and the atmosphere got very still, with no noise at all. I began to see everything as if I was hovering over the scene, above all the chaos. From my bird's-eye view, I saw Tommy, Bubba, and the tools that had been strewn about the yard. The pickax, the shovel, the square, even the crowbar, and pieces of broken cinder blocks lying about. I saw the entire scene, but one person I did not see: I didn't see myself.

The experience lasted only a few seconds, but it is something I will never forget. I am still unable to explain it. When it ended abruptly, I was right back on the front line again. I could hear Tommy's cursing and yelling, and the tools crashing all around me. I had escaped for mere seconds, but whatever happened during that time had renewed my strength. I kept fighting.

Looking back, I'm now convinced that I experienced something supernatural, perhaps an angelic visitation, a spiritual encounter of some sort, or some other indication of God's presence. Scripture says, "No testing has overtaken you that is not common to everyone. God is faithful, and he will not let you be tested beyond your strength, but with the testing he will also provide the way out so that you may be able to endure it" (1 Corinthians 10:13). Maybe God saw that I had reached a point of no strength, where I could not take any more, and He graciously gave me a brief respite. At the exact moment when I thought I couldn't last another second, I did. God made a temporary way of escape. He renewed my energy. Although it was momentary, it was enough.

I returned to the battle and continued struggling hard against Tommy. He shoved me and used both hands to swing at me. Amid all the pushing and shoving, I yelled again to Bubba, "Run! Get away from here. Leave and don't come back!" I didn't care where he went, so long as he escaped the danger. I kept lunging at Tommy with all of my might, still convinced I might get him to the ground. But I couldn't. Finally he became so irritated he grabbed me by the throat, attempting to lift me off the ground and choke me. I could feel his strong hands wrenching against my larynx and cutting off my ability to swallow and to breathe. This was one of his most dangerous moves—one I had become familiar with over the years. It was usually his last-ditch effort to silence me.

It didn't last long, though, because I was fighting back ferociously, flailing my arms and kicking at him with all I had within me. While his inebriated condition didn't decrease his strength, it most definitely decreased his ability to aim, so when he tried to hit me, I wriggled out of his grasp. To my surprise, he didn't pursue me; he simply spewed a litany of profanity in my direction.

But to my horror, I realized again, I was not his target this dreadful day. I was merely an obstacle impeding his progress; I was in the way of his target. He had his mind set on destroying the one person who was the most faithful and loyal to him. The one who truly loved him, always did what he was told, and didn't talk back. The one who was crying out and pleading for the madness to end. Our eldest child was in the path of this catastrophic storm, and by all indications, he was about to suffer a direct hit.

Tommy retrieved the pickax, again swinging it wildly through the air and yelling how he was going to use it on our son's head. Tommy seemed no longer human but appeared to have morphed into something evil and devoid of any rational thought.

My own thoughts raced: *How have I gone so long forgiving Tommy's fits and allowing him to bully our family the way he does? How could I live with myself if he ever killed one our children?*

I'd had it. I wanted out and didn't care what I had to do to make it happen. I was tired of defending myself and the kids. I was ready to end this battle once and for all!

The chase was back on, and I yelled for Bubba to run away yet again. Finally, at about two o'clock in the afternoon, as if in reluctant acquiescence to all my pleading, Bubba took off running to the front of our house. He ran down Piney Road toward the home of Patsy Wisdom and her husband, Buttermilk—two of the few neighbors our family members knew. Tommy had already polished off nearly three-quarters of a liquor bottle and was still grousing in the back of the house. Momentarily relieved to see that Bubba had disappeared somewhere, I leaned over with my hands on my knees, tried to catch my breath, and struggled not to collapse.

Tommy, however, had spotted Bubba running toward the front of the house and down Piney Road. He rushed over and fired up his Harley right away. I followed him, yelling, "What are you going to do?"

"I'm going to kill him!" Tommy yelled over the rumble of the Harley's motor. "I'm gonna find him and run over him. That's what I'm going to do." He revved the engine and took off after Bubba on his motorcycle, roaring out the driveway at full throttle.

I ran to my car, nervously pushed the key into the ignition, slammed the gearshift into drive, and stomped on the gas pedal. The car lurched forward, and I headed down the driveway too. Tommy was flying by now; I guessed by looking at my own speedometer that Tommy must have been going at least eighty miles per hour, leaving precious little time for me to catch up. But I kept the pedal to the floor, and eventually, I caught sight of him. I was determined to intercept him any way possible, even if that meant ramming his new motorcycle. In the meantime, I prayed he would lose control and crash.

As I drove, my eyes searched the sparse, low brush along the road for any sign of our son. There were few places for him to hide, so I was somewhat relieved that I didn't see him. I assumed he must be hiding in the woods someplace, otherwise his dad or I would have spotted him. Tommy raced to the end of Piney Road and turned sharply, reversing course, then sped off again back toward our home. He nearly laid his motorcycle over on its side as he made the fast hairpin turn. He churned the loose gravel on the road, but never lost control. I noted that even while drunk, he could control a speeding motorcycle—but not his raging temper.

As I followed him back to the house, I scanned each side of the road again. I breathed a bit easier when neither of us found Bubba.

Tommy pulled the Harley around to the back of the house. He was so intoxicated he could hardly stand, yet somehow he success-fully parked his bike and retreated to a spot on the back patio.

I watched him from a distance, uncertain as to what his next move might be. I couldn't be sure, but it looked to me that Tommy was finally wearing down. With Bubba gone, my main focus was keeping Tommy controlled until he passed out. I knew from past experiences that this was his normal pattern after drinking so heavily. But apparently, he wasn't finished yet. As Tommy sat on the cinder block patio wall he had built to one day accommodate a hot tub, he swayed back and forth and drank more whiskey. "Tim!" he shouted to our fifteen-year-old son. "Where are you? Get out here."

Slim, lean, bespectacled, and strong for his size, yet not as strong as Bubba, Timothy did not delay in obeying his dad when he heard his voice.

"Here I am, Dad," he said almost sheepishly, stepping outside through the basement door where the altercation had begun.

As though nothing unusual had happened, Tommy barked orders at Timothy. "Get some wood. Board up that door," he demanded. He pointed at the broken windowpane, the glass that had shattered when Bubba slammed the door.

"Yes, sir," Timothy said quietly. He went to work, gathering some boards and nailing them across the hole where the window had been. Timothy knew the routine. Every time Tommy broke a window or door around our house, he did not replace it; he simply boarded it up. The nearly empty jug of whiskey sat close by Tommy, reminding me of my plea earlier that morning that he not drink.

My eyes were swollen from crying, but as I neared the house, I saw a sight that caused more tears to well. Earlier that morning, in my haste to protect Bubba, I had told our nine-year-old daughter, Tayler, to stay inside the house amid the chaos. She had obediently done so, but as I looked up at the kitchen window, I saw her looking back down at me. I could see the fear in her face, and I wanted to run to her and hug her tightly to comfort her—but I had to deal with her father first. Tayler being safely out of harm's way was the best I could hope for in that moment.

Timothy continued boarding up the door as his dad demanded. As I drew closer, I knew I had to be careful how I spoke to Tommy. I could easily provoke another battle. Making him angrier was not smart, so I was ready to choose my words carefully. But I needn't have worried. He was not interested in my words.

When he saw me near, he stood up from the cinder block wall and glared at me. "Get into the car," he said brusquely.

For reasons I still can't explain, I did not argue; I simply did what he said. "You drive," he demanded. I slid behind the wheel and turned slightly toward him, looking at the monster in the seat next to me. Where had the kind, loving man I had married gone? I had no idea where he wanted us to go, but I pressed the accelerator and drove down our driveway toward the main road.

"Keep going," he said gruffly. "I want to get some gasoline so I can burn the house down."

What?

Why I didn't slam on the brakes and catapult him through the windshield, I'll never know. But I didn't. Instead, I drove in the direction of Self's Market, the nearby convenience store where we usually filled our vehicles with gasoline. My actions were completely irrational.

My body was so fatigued, and my mind was numb to nearly everything that came from Tommy's mouth—so, similar to most victims of abuse, I didn't argue back. Besides, in my desperation, I thought: *This could turn out well.* First responders would respond to the flames at our house—without me even calling them! I was already planning how I could get the kids out in time, and Tommy could do whatever he wanted.

We pulled in at the store, and while he pumped gasoline into his five-gallon gas can, I went inside to pay. I had been to this store many times previously, and although Tommy had severely curtailed my social interaction with folks in the community, people recognized me at that store. They knew where we lived. I wanted so badly to plead for help, but I didn't. My thoughts raced. *How does he have this much control over me?* I stood right in front of the counter and the clerk, yet I didn't dare utter a word about Tommy's actions.

I was terrified of what Tommy might do to us, and he knew it. In fact, the fear of what *was* happening seemed more tolerable than the fear of what *could* happen. The fear of the unknown was always far greater to me. Besides, I figured no one could help us to the degree we needed. A patrol car pulling up to the house would only put us at a greater risk. What the kids and I needed was a long-term safety plan. But I didn't know how to get that sort of help without putting us all in jeopardy. I still cringed every time I recalled how I had suffered brutally for calling the police years before.

Still, the way Tommy had threatened our son for hours and the gruesome, grotesque words he had shouted at him were impossible to unhear. How could a father speak like that to his own son? The rage behind his shouting came from a deep, dark hole somewhere inside him.

At the same time, the level of pain I felt as a mother unable to shield her son from such hurt was indescribable. Tommy had terrorized our family and me for years, but this day was different. He was more unpredictable than ever, more erratic, more of his worst self than usual—and that was saying something. I knew the children and I could no longer stay with this monster, no matter the outcome of this horrible day. I needed to figure out how to escape—but I had no time to think. Appeasing Tommy any way I could was my priority and my only hope in the moment. I kept reminding myself, *In the past, after wild fits, he has been regretful. Then he has begged for forgiveness.* That was what I was waiting for— hoping and praying for. That's when I would get out.

But those expressions of remorse were much further from Tommy's lips, mind, and heart than I could have imagined.

CHAPTER 29

Dad Won't Hurt Us Anymore

Tommy and I returned from the store, and he got out of the car to retrieve the full can of gas from the trunk. I was still sitting in the driver's seat when I looked in my rearview mirror and saw him standing behind the car in front of the trunk. Since I had not yet shut off the car's engine, it suddenly occurred to me: *I can run him over!*

It was an outrageous idea, but without a second thought, my eyes moved from the mirror to the gearshift. My shaking hand shifted the car into reverse. All I had to do was stomp on the gas pedal, and it would be over in a matter of seconds. I trembled as I took one last glance in the mirror to ensure Tommy was still in sight. He was.

But then, just as I prepared to hit the pedal, Timothy suddenly came into view and stood right next to his dad. I jerked my foot away, slammed the gearshift into park, shut off the car, and jumped out. My stomach roiled as I pondered what had almost happened, and I fought off the urge to vomit.

Tommy took the gas can to the back porch and set it down near the door, but he did not splash any gasoline around the premises.

He seemed disoriented, and since I had no idea what he might do next, I closely watched his every move. He went back down to the basement level of the house, where many of his tools lay in a tangled mess. Looking somewhat discombobulated, he fumbled around for a while, trying to fix broken pieces of tools. Then he went inside and sat down at the kitchen table. I followed him from a distance, but he knew I was there.

"Make me a sandwich," he barked at me.

"A sandwich," I repeated, more to myself than to him. "All right, just a minute." I couldn't believe he wanted to eat after his disgusting behavior, but at least he had calmed down. Maybe after he ate, he would get tired and lie down. Perfect. I knew where he had placed the gas can, and I planned to hide it when he wasn't paying attention.

I found Timmy and Tayler and quietly told them to go downstairs and hide under their beds until it was safe.

While I made his sandwich, Tommy sat in his chair, staring into space and mumbling incoherently. "Hurry up!" he snapped. "Do you hear me?" I looked at him and nodded my head. He was trying to open his medication bottles when I placed his plate in front of him. He never missed a dose. Despite all that had happened that day, he was acting as though everything was normal—so of course it was time to take his pills before he ate. "Open these medicine bottles," he barked. The childproof caps were more than he could manage in his current condition. I opened the caps, placed the bottles near his plate, and returned to the kitchen.

When he went to the bathroom, I ran down to the basement to check on the kids. Anytime I stepped out of Tommy's sight, he bellowed my name until I returned to the room—so he was yelling for me before I got back up the stairs. He staggered down the hallway toward the bedroom doorway. "Come help me take these boots off," he demanded. "I want to lie down for a while, but I'm gonna be listening for that boy's footsteps." Tommy glowered at me. "And when he comes back, he's dead. I'm killing him."

I desperately tried not to show shock on my face or to respond in any way.

Finally! I thought. *He's going to sleep. This is what I have been waiting on for several hours.*

I knelt down in front of him and unlaced his muddy boots. As I tugged at them, he berated me and told me what a terrible wife I was for taking up for that "mama's boy."

It took all the self-control within me to hold my tongue. I said very little to him in those moments. I mumbled what he wanted to hear, hoping he might apologize as he had done so many times previously. This was usually the point when he would start crying and beg for forgiveness. But not this time. Tommy slouched down on his back on the mattress. I knew he wouldn't be able to sleep that way, since he suffered from sleep apnea and couldn't breathe lying down without the help of a CPAP machine. So I moved the machine closer to his head. I thought he couldn't get any meaner, but he did. He continued to grumble obscenities from the bed.

I wanted him to sleep. At least the kids and I would be out of immediate danger while he slept off the booze. I quietly slipped out of our bedroom and walked toward the front of the house. I was barely down the hallway when Tommy yelled again, wanting to know my whereabouts. "Don't think I'm sleeping. I'm not. I'm *waiting.*"

His words sent chills up my neck. I knew what his words meant. I also knew that if I did not respond and say something to placate his suspicions, I risked him getting out of bed and looking for me.

I quickly shouted back toward the bedroom, "Okay!"

He did not respond further, so for the moment, we were safe.

I quietly walked over to the phone to make some calls, hoping I could track down Bubba's whereabouts. The phone was a landline, the only one we had in the house, and I tried to be particularly cagey so Tommy couldn't hear me. I felt sure Bubba had run to the home of our neighbors, Patsy and Buttermilk Wisdom, so the first call I made was to them. I wanted to make sure Bubba knew it was not safe for him to come back home yet. My head was throbbing, my body ached, and my eyes were swollen. I struggled to think quickly and clearly while I had this opportunity.

Patsy and Buttermilk Wisdom were friendly, salt-of-the-earth folks who had lived in Lawrenceburg for years. The whole community knew them, and they knew everyone in town. A balding, jovial, full-faced type of fellow, Buttermilk could be found wearing denim overalls without fail. His gregarious wife, Patsy, had never met a stranger, and since she could talk a person's ear off, she and I naturally became friends—at least, as close of friends as Tommy allowed. The Wisdoms had children near our kids' ages, and the family was kind to our children, so it wouldn't surprise me if Bubba had fled to their nearby farm.

I hurriedly dialed the Wisdoms' phone number. Patsy answered, and I whispered into the phone's mouthpiece, "Miss Patsy, is Bubba over there?"

"Why, yes! Yes, he is," Patsy responded in her normal, gregarious manner.

I didn't have time to be circumspect, so I cut right to the chase. "Patsy, please keep Bubba there as long as you can. It is not safe for him to come home."

"Ah, yes," Patsy said, as though trying to keep someone from being alarmed. "I see. Yes. I will do my best."

"May I speak with him, please?" I asked.

"Of course. Just a moment," she replied. "Bubba!" I heard her call. "It's your mother on the line. She wants to talk with you."

Moments later, Bubba was on the phone. "Mom," he said somberly, "are you okay?"

"Yes, Bubba, I'm okay," I said. "And so is everyone else. But it is not safe for you to come home yet. Your dad just now went into the bedroom." I spoke more quietly. "This is bad, Bubba. Worse than usual."

"Is Dad still mad? Has he calmed down yet?"

"Not really. He's still yelling from the bedroom."

Bubba seemed to sense the fear in my voice.

"Bubba, please. Under no circumstances should you come home right now. Stay right where you are."

"Mom, listen—"

"Bubba! Please don't argue with me. Just stay where you are. He'll fall asleep soon, and you know how that goes. Just stay there with Patsy and Buttermilk for a while."

I didn't want to tell Bubba that I planned for us to leave. He didn't need that extra burden on him yet. I simply wanted him to remain safe. I knew that if he came home before Tommy had slept off the booze, World War III would start all over again.

"I need to go check on Timmy and Tayler. I love you."

I couldn't risk Tommy hearing me on the phone, so I hung up quickly. I breathed a bit easier knowing that Bubba was safe at the Wisdoms' home. His father was still awake and listening from the bedroom, calling out profanely to me every few minutes to make sure I knew he was still in control.

I quietly slipped downstairs and found Timothy and Tayler hiding under their beds, just as I had asked them to do earlier. Timothy had his hands wrapped tightly around one of Tommy's rifles. Although his dad had taught him how to use a gun for hunting, it scared me to see Timothy clutching the weapon so tenaciously. Still, I was glad the younger kids were relatively safe.

"Just stay here a little longer," I whispered to them. "Your dad will be sleeping soon, then it will be safe to come out." I hurried back upstairs before Tommy could realize I had been gone.

Back in the kitchen, amid a few moments of relative calm and quietness, I forced my mind to consider our possible escape plans. *Think. Think! How can we get out of here?* I was afraid to call anyone for help, but more afraid to stay. What if we could just disappear? *If we leave, we have to be together,* I thought. That meant I'd have to pick up Tonie Jo from her friend's home, and Bubba from the Wisdoms'. *There will be no second chance with Tommy. If I leave with the kids, there is no coming back.*

It was now around six o'clock in the evening, and as I stood at the kitchen sink pondering my options, I heard the front door open. My heart nearly jumped from my chest as I turned and saw Bubba slowly coming through the open doorway!

Nooooo! I fought to squelch any sound escaping from my mouth. I bounded across the room like a deer in what seemed like one giant leap, then pushed my hands against Bubba's chest. "No, Bubba!" I whispered frantically. "Don't come any further. You can't come in. It's too soon. You can't stay. Don't dare come back yet."

"Where's Dad?" Bubba asked quietly. "Is he passed out yet?"

"He's in bed, but he's not sleeping," I barely whispered.

"Is he still mad?" Bubba asked.

"Yes!" I whispered fiercely, trying to make sure Bubba understood the danger he was in. "You need to go, Bubba. Get away from here for a while."

Bubba looked at me kindly and said, "I'm not leaving you and the kids again, Mom."

"Bubba!"

"No, Mom. I'm not leaving," he repeated. "I was worried about you and Timmy and Tayler the whole time I was gone. I'm staying right here."

Our firstborn son sat down resolutely on a chair, right near the front door. I could tell by the look in his eyes that he was not going to leave.

Fear gripped me, knowing his dad was only a few yards away. He had just called my name shortly before Bubba had come inside. Tommy typically would have passed out by now—but he hadn't. And Bubba seemed to understand the seriousness, but he had decided that leaving again was not an option.

Bubba and I continued talking in terse whispers as I told him how his dad had threatened to burn the house down. Then I told him how I had nearly run over Timmy with the car. I was an emotional wreck. "I don't think this fight has ended yet, Bubba. So please, just go hide somewhere."

"No, I'm not leaving," he replied quietly.

I knew I had to act. It was only a matter of time before Tommy was up and looking for me. Once he discovered that Bubba was back, things would escalate again—that much I knew. I also recognized that I could not and would not leave my son alone with his insane father. *Only over my dead body will Tommy ever lay another hand on Bubba*, I said to myself.

My mind went to the kids downstairs, still hiding under their beds. I left Bubba sitting in the chair and slipped downstairs to check on them. Tayler was huddled under a bed, paralyzed by fear, and Timmy was still hugging the rifle under his bed. "Come on out," I whispered, waving to them. "But be very quiet." I took the gun from Timmy and set it in the hallway, then hustled our two younger children out of the house through the downstairs back door. I was uncertain how long the respite would last, or if Tommy would suddenly erupt again.

As I guided them out of the house, I looked up and saw Tonie Jo and her friend coming down the driveway in the friend's pickup truck. The friend was dropping her off after a rare overnight visit. As soon as Tonie Jo hopped out of the truck, I made eye contact with her and put my finger to my lips. "Shhhhh!"

Almost instinctively, it seemed, Tonie Jo understood something was wrong. She stopped in the driveway, turned to her friend, and spoke to her. They hugged in the driveway, and her friend turned the truck around and headed back out the lane. Tonie Jo continued toward the back of our house, where I paced nervously with Tayler and Timothy.

I had no time to explain to Tonie Jo, but when she saw my tearstained face and my disheveled gray jogging outfit, she read between the lines. She could tell we were in trouble.

"Quickly, kids," I implored them, "run into the woods and don't come back for a while." Our closest neighbors were at least a football field's length away, so I considered the woods the safest place for the three younger kids.

"But it's going to get dark out here, Mom," Tonie Jo pointed out. She did not seem to be looking for a reason to reject my instructions—just emphasizing the unusual aspect of my request.

"I'm cold," Tayler added.

"I know, I know," I said, glancing back toward the house. I didn't want them anywhere near the house and knew the woods would be the safest place for them. I had to get back inside with Bubba. If his dad got up and found him there, it would all be over.

"Just stay outside for a while," I said. "Stay in the woods."

But the kids were all crying and begging me not to make them leave. I pleaded for them to run and hide and even tried to shoo them off in the direction of the woods, but they were afraid and getting more so by the minute. My mind went back to Bubba sitting inside the house. I knew I had to get back in there.

"Okay, okay. Come over here and sit inside your dad's pickup truck," I said, pushing them in the direction of the parked vehicle nearby. "I'll be back as soon as I can." I hustled the kids into Tommy's truck and shut the door, making sure not to slam it.

I turned around and headed back toward the house. When I looked up, I saw Bubba slowly and somberly walking toward me, coming out of the basement door. He carried a long-barreled rifle in his hand.

The last time Bubba had picked up a gun to protect us from one of Tommy's blistering and abusive rampages, Tommy had forced Bubba to spend the night outside in the cold. Tommy had warned him, "If you ever point a gun at me again, you'd better make sure it is loaded!" Tommy's taunting words still haunted me.

So far, the events of this day had been even worse than *that* day's, so I wasn't completely surprised to see Bubba carrying the rifle. Besides, I figured he had found the gun I had taken away from Timmy. I had left it in the hallway, so I thought he might be bringing the rifle to me so I could protect the kids. I hadn't been inside for several minutes, and I knew if Tommy came out of the bedroom, he would be looking for me. Having a weapon might not be a bad idea.

The other kids tumbled out of the truck and gathered around me as I started walking toward Bubba. When Bubba and I were within earshot of each other, only a few feet apart, he approached me and spoke, but I could barely hear what he was saying. His face was expressionless, devoid of tears, and his voice was a whisper. He said something again, but this time he moved his face next to mine and spoke quietly in my ear.

"I shot him," Bubba said.

I stared back at him, stunned.

"Mom, I shot Dad."

I heard what our son was saying, but my brain couldn't process the words. Or perhaps I didn't believe what I was hearing.

Still fearful, confused, and concerned for Bubba, I said, "Keep the gun beside you for your protection."

Bubba slowly shook his head from side to side. "I shot him, Mom. He's gone." Then as if to make sure I understood, he looked directly at me and said, "Mom, Dad's dead."

My eyes grew wide in shock as I tried to comprehend Bubba's words.

Bubba said softly, "Dad's not going to hurt us anymore, Mom."

CHAPTER 30

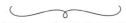

Incarceration

M y body was exhausted, and my mind was numb from the events of the day—so Bubba's words were still not computing. "Come with me, Mom," Bubba said. "I'll show you."

The three younger children were still huddled together in the yard near Tommy's truck. I turned to them and said, "Go to the front porch, kids. Stay right there till I come back. Don't come into the house."

Bubba and I walked back up the steps and through the door of the house. It was quiet inside except for one telltale sound—the steady low-toned humming of Tommy's CPAP machine. It was still running, but it was not rising and falling as it would if Tommy were breathing. Tommy had used the machine regularly since gaining so much weight. Without it, he couldn't sleep on his back. I had heard the sound of that machine every night for several years, so I knew if the machine was not functioning, neither was Tommy.

I did not have to go into the room to know Tommy was dead.

"We have to call the police," I said to Bubba.

"I know, Mom," he replied somberly.

I went to the phone, but before I dialed 911, I said, "I'm going to call Patsy and Buttermilk first."

I called Patsy and said, "I need to talk to you bad…I need you to come to the house." I explained briefly what had happened, and Patsy gasped on the phone. She knew Tommy and Bubba had been at odds earlier that day because Bubba, shirtless and barefoot, had fled to her home for a refuge from his father's assaults. But she had no idea of the seriousness of it all.

The kids and I were waiting on the front porch when Patsy arrived. She and Buttermilk lived about two miles away from us, so she arrived in a matter of minutes. When Patsy pulled to a stop in our driveway, I got into her truck and told her what had happened.

She nodded. "All right," she said. "Tell the kids to get into the truck. I'll be right back." Patsy went into the house by herself to check out the situation.

She walked down the hall to the bedroom and found Tommy, right where Bubba had shot him. Tommy lay face up, fully clothed except for his boots, dead in the bed. Patsy later told me that she cursed him before turning around and walking away. She came out, got in the truck, and drove us to her house, where she called the police to report the crime.

Within minutes, the police cars roared down Piney Road on their way to the scene of the homicide. Patsy had done her best to describe what had happened, but the officers were wary nonetheless.

About the same time, other police officers arrived at Patsy and Buttermilk's home. The officers questioned Bubba and me for a few minutes before laying some legal police statement pads in front of Bubba, Timmy, and me. "Write down everything you can remember," a female officer instructed. "Start right at the beginning." It was nearly eight o'clock at night, and we were all exhausted—but we sat at Patsy's table and began to write what we remembered.

It all seemed to be happening in blurry slow motion, but I dutifully tried to recall how the events of the day had transpired. It ripped my heart out even to put the words down on the notepad.

Interestingly, without comparing notes, both Bubba and I began our statements with Tommy drinking heavily, starting early in the morning. In his own remarkably controlled expressions, Bubba printed, "Starting this morning, Dad started drinking; he was drinking oversized shots of whiskey. He started yelling at me while we were working…then he took a framing square and tried to cut my head off. I picked up a small steel pan and tried blocking myself. After dodging the square, he started running after me. That's when I threw the metal pan at him and ran to the door and slammed it, breaking the glass…"

Bubba wrote about running to Patsy and Buttermilk's house. Then, picking up the story later that day, he wrote, "I was so afraid and scared for my mama and the kids, so I ran back to the house. That's when Mama said Dad was going to kill me so we talked outside and Mama was very scared for me and for the kids. So I had enough and went and got my .22 Long Rifle and shot him in his head. Then I went back outside and told my mom that everything was going to be all right and that I shot Dad. I didn't tell the other kids about what I did and my mom was outside crying when I did it…she didn't know about it."

Fifteen-year-old Timmy's statement was equally poignant. Timmy, too, told about Tommy yelling and cussing at Bubba and throwing the carpenter's square at him. He also remembered Bubba trying to defend himself with the stainless steel pan before finally throwing it at Tommy and bolting for the door. "My dad… got mad and started running after my brother and [threw] things at him. Then he [threatened] to chop off his head with a pickax. My mom told me to go inside with my sister. Then she, me, and my sister were looking out the window and saw my dad telling my brother to come down and fight. He picked up a level and acted like he was going to hit him, then my brother started to leave and went to a friend's house."

Once we had written our statements, the police officers indicated that it was time for us to go. Buttermilk found a shirt and some shoes that Bubba could wear to the sheriff's department in Lawrenceburg.

Timmy, Tonie Jo, and Tayler stayed with Buttermilk, but the police handcuffed Bubba and took him in their squad car to the police station. Patsy and I followed behind in a separate vehicle.

Patsy and I pulled in right behind the squad car. The officers guided Bubba and me inside, where we stood together for a few minutes. Then officers took us into different rooms for questioning. I didn't know any better, but I probably could have protested the police separating us. But I assumed they'd have us sign some sort of documents, and that would be it. By now, two friends from church, Melissa Brazier and Gail Dixon, and some other friends had arrived at the police station to be with us.

One of the officers asked me about the red marks around my neck. I was not even aware of the welts where Tommy had tried to choke me. Another female officer grilled me about the blood on my clothes. I hadn't really noticed that, either, but when I looked at my jogging suit, I was surprised to see blood all over me.

"Whose blood is that?" the officer asked.

I looked at my hands and didn't see any wounds. I was bruised and sore, but I didn't think I was bleeding. Suddenly I realized where the blood had come from. "Oh, I'm okay," I told the officer. "This is not my blood. This is my husband's blood!"

That was probably not the best answer, but I was simply being honest. And to the credit of the police, they may have thought I was the aggressor; they had no reason to believe me, even though Bubba had already admitted to pulling the trigger. But they had no real way of knowing the truth apart from Bubba's word and mine. On the other hand, they did not take any blood samples from my clothes, nor do I recall them taking any photos of the red marks around my neck.

They tested both Bubba's hands and mine for black gunpowder residue. That seemed unnecessary to me since Bubba and I had told them from the beginning that *he* had shot his dad.

I naïvely thought that after we explained what had happened, and why Bubba had shot his dad, that both Bubba and I would be returning home from the police station that night. I could not imagine anyone doubting the veracity of our report. I thought they would simply be happy we had survived. But that was not the way things worked. The officers escorted Bubba to a cell inside the jail, and I was told to go home. "When's Bubba coming home?" I asked.

"We'll let you know," an officer said. "He will be at the juvenile detention center until his arraignment." Although they assured me he would be safe, I was terrified. According to the police report, they transported Bubba to the Maury County Detention Center at 11:07 p.m. It was still Good Friday, but I was having a hard time remembering what was so good about it.

Leaving the police station under a cloud of suspicion was difficult enough. Leaving my seventeen-year-old son in the custody of the police was even more heartrending. I had no idea when I would see him next. Nor could I imagine what he might experience alone in jail, behind bars for protecting his family from near-certain death. I wanted this nightmare to be over for him—and in some ways, it was; but in many other ways, it was just beginning.

Bubba was facing first-degree murder charges, so upon his arrival at the juvenile detention center, he was strip-searched, dressed in an orange prison jumpsuit, and shackled at the hands and feet. He would be kept there for three days, then moved for four weeks of mental evaluation in Chattanooga. But I did not know that yet. That night, I was still hoping to bring him home the following day, after the police had finished their investigation.

Oddly enough, the police did not confiscate my blood-splattered clothing as evidence. I would have gladly given it to them. I couldn't wait to get out of that mess.

While the police still combed the grounds, I gathered some fresh clothes from our house. Then I returned to Patsy and Buttermilk's home, where I talked briefly with the kids. "Do you know what happened to Daddy?" I asked Tayler as I helped her get a bath. "Yeah," she said. "Daddy's at jail. He did a lot of bad things. Daddy's at jail."

"Well, actually, he's not," I said. "Bubba shot and killed your dad."

Tayler didn't cry; she showed little emotion. "Can I just get my bath and go play with Brianna?" (Patsy and Buttermilk's daughter).

I went to talk with Timmy and Tonie Jo. Timmy was quiet. He already knew what had happened, having overheard Bubba first telling me what he had done. Tonie Jo had thought her dad had gone to jail, but Brianna had told her otherwise. So both of the kids had some understanding of the tragedy before I explained anything to them. Whether they felt shock or relief, they were solemn but did not seem overly distraught at the news.

I asked to take a shower. Once in the bathroom, I peeled the bloody athletic jogging suit off my bruised body. I didn't give the clothes to Patsy to wash but saved them in case the police asked for them. I kept them for several years before eventually destroying them.

My next challenge was to call Tommy's mom and dad and tell them their grandson had shot and killed their son. "I have to call Pastor Tom and Sally," I told Patsy. I knew Pap and Granny cared about the kids and me, and regardless of Tommy's impulsive and erratic behavior, he was still their son.

Patsy understood my nervousness. "Go on into our bedroom," she said. "There's a phone in there. Take as long as you need."

I went into the bedroom and dialed Pap and Granny's telephone number in Florida. I could feel my heart beating faster and harder. *How can I deliver this awful news to my mother- and father-in-law?* I sat down on the floor at the foot of Buttermilk and Patsy's bed. Pap answered the phone in his strong, soothing manner.

I greeted him briefly but then blurted out what had happened. "Tommy was upset; he was mad; he was trying to hurt us..." I paused, trying desperately to maintain some sense of composure. "Bubba tried to run, and Tommy kept chasing him. He was threatening to kill Bubba...so Bubba shot him."

Poor Pap. The words tumbled out of me like Niagara Falls, barely offering him a chance to respond or ask questions. I can't imagine how my message crushed his dear heart.

Pap stopped me. His voice was quiet. "Sandee Jo, is Tommy alive?" he asked.

"No," I said sadly.

I tried to explain more to Pastor Schankweiler, but everything was still a blur—and though I tried hard to have a coherent conversation, the words tumbled out and I could feel myself rambling.

"So Bubba and Tommy had a fight?" he asked calmly.

"Yes, sir," I answered.

"And that fight got out of hand?"

"Yes, sir."

"And at some point, Bubba picked up a gun and shot his dad?"

"Yes, sir."

"And Tommy is dead?"

"Yes, sir. He is." We both were straining to find words, so after a few more terse sentences, we hung up. I felt sure his heart was breaking, yet I did not feel any condemnation from the pastor—only a deep, unconditional love and an unspeakable sadness. I grieved with him, knowing the horrific news he was about to pass on to my mother-in-law.

∽◦⧜◦∾

My head was splitting with the worst headache I'd ever felt. All I wanted was to go to bed, and hopefully upon waking, discover that the events of Good Friday had all been a bad dream. I tried to sleep at Patsy and Buttermilk's home, but mostly I tossed and turned all night long, reliving the awful events of the day and worrying that Bubba was experiencing a similar night—or worse.

The next day, I woke with the same splitting headache. Patsy told her daughter Misty, "I'm going over to clean up the house, and you drive Sandee Jo to the Nashville airport. Her mom is coming in from Tampa."

Misty tried to talk with me as we drove, but I was numb. I sat in the passenger's seat and stared out the window at the passing scenery. Exhausted, I closed my eyes in semi-sleep. We found Mom at the airport, and I just hugged her. I didn't try to explain anything to her. I had been strong for so many years, and now I was weak and worn-out. In my mother's embrace, however, I felt safe. I no longer had to pretend to be strong. She got in the front seat, and I got in the back. Then I slept most of the way back to Lawrenceburg. I vaguely heard Mom and Misty talking in low tones, as Misty tried to fill her in on what she knew.

The police officers permitted Patsy to scrub and clean my house before Misty, my mom, and I returned from Nashville. When we walked back inside the house that afternoon, Patsy had done such a thorough cleaning, it was impossible to tell that anything awful had happened there. There was no sign of blood, and she had changed the bed linens. Mom said, "Why don't you go lie down? I'll take care of the kids." She didn't have to make that suggestion twice. My head was still pounding, but I felt safe. I could take a nap without fear.

As I closed the bedroom door, I noticed the four Easter baskets I had prepared for the kids prior to Good Friday. They were still hidden behind the door where I had left them. I had planned to place them on the dining room table before leaving for work on Easter Sunday morning. I had imagined the kids' excitement as they discovered all the candy and treats.

I took the Easter baskets out and placed them on the table where the kids could find them. When they came home from Patsy and Buttermilk's, the treats were there waiting for them. They devoured the goodies in each of their baskets, but none of the kids touched anything from Bubba's basket. We kept it right there on the table and didn't move it, even long after the other baskets were empty. Tayler especially guarded her big brother's basket, so it would be perfect for him when he arrived home. We could not have imagined that the basket would remain on the table for more than five weeks.

I was still physically and emotionally exhausted. I lay down that afternoon to take a nap and didn't awaken until morning. I realized it was the first time I had slept peacefully in ages. I got out of bed a couple of times but went straight back and crawled under the covers again. Mom and I slept there that night in what had been the bedroom I shared with Tommy.

When I awakened the next day, I learned that Pap and Granny were on their way to Tennessee from Florida. I worried they would be accusatory toward me, that they might assume Tommy's death was my fault. *How will they react?* I fretted. I sat on my bed looking out the window, worrying. Would they feel anger? Disgust? Disdain? I had no idea.

But when they came through the door, Granny hurried to me and threw her arms around me in an emotional embrace. Words were not necessary. We wept together. Pap remained calm and stoic, but his eyes welled with tears. I could tell he, too, was deeply moved. Granny and Pap stayed close by until Tommy's memorial service.

Granny and I worked through most of the funeral arrangements. Since Tommy and our family had lived in Lawrenceburg for two years, we wanted an opportunity to celebrate his life among our friends there, which we did at Deerfield Baptist Church on March 26, 2008. But most of Tommy's life had been lived in Florida, so we decided to have a second memorial at his home church in Avon Park. Tommy's dad, Pastor Schankweiler, would lead both services for his son.

Following the shooting, our church family in Lawrenceburg showed us unconditional love and support. They brought food to the house, and more importantly, prayed for us constantly. I felt their prayers buoying us up as one wave of emotion after another rolled over us. Pastor Tony Gordy and our friends Gail Dixon and Melissa Brazier kept the congregation informed of our needs, and though I had next to nothing in my checking account on the day of the tragedy, our family never went without. God's true servants took care of us.

CHAPTER 31

Finding a Lawyer

My friends from church gave me the names of good attorneys I might wish to speak with. I didn't know any of the lawyers on their list and had no clue how to start the process. Worse yet, it was Easter weekend. I had little hope of finding an attorney, but I dialed the telephone number of the first name listed. As I heard the phone ringing, I wondered, *How do I even begin a conversation like this?*

A voice answered the phone, "Hello. Daniel Freeman." I stumbled through the reason for my call. "I need to hire a lawyer," I said, "because my son shot and killed his dad this weekend."

Simply hearing the words coming out of my mouth was shocking.

But the attorney did not seem surprised or put off in any way. "Okay," he said. "I need you to tell me specifically what happened. Tell me all of the details."

I told him as much as I knew, and the attorney scribbled notes on a yellow legal pad as I talked. He later gave me those notes and, along with the statements Bubba, Timmy, and I wrote for the police within a few hours of the incident, they became a valuable contemporaneous account of what had happened on Good Friday.

Mr. Freeman was matter-of-fact about everything. "Okay, come into my office on Monday." He explained what his services might cost. He showed no great emotional support or compassion. He didn't even say, "I'm so sorry to hear this." He was straightforward and businesslike.

I had no idea how I was going to pay for an attorney, but the people from our church assured me they would help. And they did. Somebody from the church wrote a check so I could retain the attorney's services.

I went to meet with Attorney Daniel Freeman by myself on Monday. He was an older gentleman—the quintessential disheveled-looking lawyer, unconcerned about his personal appearance or anything other than the law. Again, he was unemotional and seemingly lacking in compassion, but he was quite good at explaining what we might be facing, even though I did not completely understand it. Freeman minced no words. "I pulled the papers on the case, and here is what we are going to do. You are claiming self-defense..."

I waited with great anticipation for Daniel Freeman to tell me something good, to give me some ray of hope that Bubba could be coming home soon.

Mr. Freeman never did.

Instead, he said, "Hmm, you are claiming self-defense, but it looks like your son might be facing first-degree murder charges." The attorney rubbed his chin with his hand and slowly shook his head from side to side. "But we'll do our best."

I left the attorney's office feeling even worse than when I went in.

Each time I met with the attorney, I expected good news. But it didn't come. The lawyer seemed especially careful not to raise my expectations of a quick resolution to Bubba's case. He explained everything, but in terms I often didn't understand. When I got back to the house, Pap asked, "What did the lawyer say?"

"I don't really know," I answered. "But people say he is good and knows what he is doing." I certainly hoped so.

⚬჻⚬

A few days later, I went to the courthouse for Bubba's official arraignment and preliminary hearing before Judge Patricia "Patty" McGuire, a judge known as a tough, hard-as-nails authority. By that time, word had gotten out—and members of the community rallied around Bubba. When the bailiff brought Bubba in, the courtroom was jammed with supporters, including some of Bubba's teachers and people from our church. The courthouse was so crowded, people spilled out onto the front lawn. Many of those in attendance had signed petitions asking Judge McGuire to grant leniency to Bubba because of the mitigating circumstances and Bubba's impeccable character.

Attorney Daniel Freeman accompanied Pap, Granny, and me into the courtroom.

The officers guided Bubba to the front of the courtroom, after which they allowed me to go to him briefly. "You can speak to him before the judge comes in," one of the officers said. Pap and Granny had to stay back. I hadn't seen Bubba since the officers had separated us on the night of Good Friday at the police station. Now he wore an orange prison jumpsuit and shackles. Two officers stood close by as I hugged him, but we didn't say much at that moment.

He sat in a chair, facing the bench where the judge would preside. I was dressed in a long black skirt with flowers and a dark top; I had my hair up rather than down, and I wore glasses rather than contact lenses. I looked like an angry mama bear on a mission, I'm sure. I knelt beside Bubba, and he looked at me.

"How are you doing, Mom?" he asked quietly.

"I'm doing okay," I said. "How about you?"

"I'm okay," he said.

That was all the time we had before Judge McGuire entered the room and the bailiff brought the proceedings to order. "All rise."

Bubba was officially charged with first-degree murder; he was not required to make any statements that day, nor was I. Judge McGuire declared that as a juvenile, Bubba must be psychologically evaluated. "We have to know his mental state of mind before we can move forward," she said. Watching the court police officers lead my seventeen-year-old son out of the room in shackles was one of the worst moments of my life. We didn't even get to say goodbye.

I got in the car thinking, *My baby is here, and I am going home.*

Bubba was returned to the juvenile detention center, where he would remain for three days. During that time, I was not permitted to visit him; I was, however, permitted to talk with him by phone, and I cherished every moment I heard his voice on the other end of the line.

CHAPTER 32

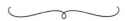

Honoring One Who Doesn't Deserve It

We held the second memorial service for Tommy on April 13, 2008, in the Avon Park church where he had grown up and worked with his dad. Tommy's father was still deeply grieving, but he would not hear of anyone else guiding the memorials for his dead son.

Walking through the house and collecting photographs to display at the funerals, as well as other items Tommy had left behind, was no easy task. Many of those items evoked strong emotions in me, few of them good. I gathered many of Tommy's personal effects and packed them up for his family.

Even though he had inflicted such horrendous pain on the kids and me over the years, the children still loved him. He was their dad, and I encouraged them to honor him as best they could. Moreover, I wanted to be sensitive to Pap and Granny and the other family members. They had come to Lawrenceburg to support and care for us while grieving their own tragic loss. I loved them and appreciated them even more.

Together with Granny and Pap, I helped plan the memorials for Tommy, arranging the photographs and suggesting the right speakers and songs for the service. I was grateful for my in-laws' help as I stumbled through the heavy, gut-wrenching process.

The memorial service in Florida drew far more people and was much more emotional than the service in Tennessee. Many friends of the Schankweiler family, people I hadn't seen in years, wanted to hug me and offer condolences. I was grateful for their support but felt somewhat stilted in my responses. The people in the Florida congregation did not know the same Tommy that I did. They knew him as a helpful, hardworking, fun-loving friend and family member, so I did my best to honor that Tommy, even though he did not deserve it. In my mind, as well as in my comments, I separated the Tommy who had died from the young Tommy I met as a teenager. The mental compartmentalization helped get me through the service, and it also helped me to better empathize with his family. I purposely did nothing to dispel their positive memories of the young man I had met at the church nearly twenty years earlier, and with whom I had fallen in love and married.

Nor did anyone else mention all the terrible things Tommy had done to the kids and me.

I knew the people in the church that day truly cared about Tommy and wanted to pay their respects and grieve along with Tommy's family members. It was a bittersweet experience for me as I listened to many deeply devout people talking about all of Tommy's wonderful virtues. I felt sadness for his family and compassion for them as they grieved the loss of Tommy. I didn't want to burst their bubbles and tell them how he had tormented the kids and me, or say anything that would disparage their memories, but I had difficulty sharing in their grief. I sat numbly at the front of the church with our children, simply hoping it would end so the children and I could return to Tennessee and move on with our lives.

When it came time for me to stand in front of the congregation, I drew inspiration from Karen Peck and New River's gospel song "Four Days Late," based on the biblical account of Lazarus, the friend of Jesus, who died. Jesus did not arrive at the tomb until Lazarus had been in the grave for four days, and Mary and Martha, his sisters, both let Jesus know He was late. If He had been there earlier, they told Him, perhaps Lazarus might still be alive.

I could relate to the song in many ways, often praying, "Lord, where are You? Why don't You do something about this horrendous situation?"

On Good Friday, the message of the song seemed especially poignant. I prayed, *God, please save us!* I didn't understand why God was not showing up for us.

Even since Tommy's death, I wondered why it had to be that way. Why could he not have died a normal death? He could easily have suffered a tragic crash on his motorcycle. Why did my teenage son have to carry this heavy burden for the rest of his life?

As Scripture and the song expressed, I felt that God was late. I knew the ending of Lazarus's story—that even after he died, Jesus raised him from the dead. But I could not imagine such a resurrection in our lives.

Bubba was unable to attend either service since he was still incarcerated in Chattanooga, undergoing psychological examinations and therapy every day at Cumberland Hall. He never really had an opportunity to say goodbye to his father once he had pulled the trigger, so he silently grieved the loss of his dad. It was an ironic, surreal set of circumstances, since his dad had been the person who had taught Bubba how to shoot a gun.

CHAPTER 33

Compassion and Protection

Although it was scary, I was almost glad when Bubba had at last been transferred to Chattanooga for mental evaluation. At least the authorities permitted visitations there, albeit only once a week for thirty minutes. I was already planning to make the drive to see my incarcerated son. He had been in a juvenile detention center for three days, and although we had brief phone conversations, I had not seen my son's face.

Making that initial phone call to Tommy's parents informing them of their son's death was difficult but necessary. They deserved to hear the sad news from me rather than someone else relaying the information. Always compassionate, Pastor Schankweiler was devastated but had responded with grace and kindness. He and Sally promised to come be with the kids and me, which they did. But they did even more.

Three weeks after the shooting, the house next to ours was put up for sale. The couple who lived there told police that they had heard an awful commotion from across the pasture on Good Friday, but they didn't have any idea what was going on. How much knowledge they had of the horrific scene, and whether what had happened influenced their decision to move, I don't know. But in an unusual way, their leaving worked to the kids' and my advantage.

Within days of Tommy's death, Pap gently broached an awkward subject. "Will you and the kids move back to Florida?" he asked.

"No, I don't think so...at least not yet," I replied. "I'd like to move back to Florida eventually, but the kids have school and friends here, and a strong network of support at our church, so I don't want to take them away from that."

"Well, we'd like to come there and help you with the kids," Pap said. Life was such a blur, I thought he meant they planned to visit frequently, and I was most grateful. But Granny and Pap had a bigger plan.

Pastor and Mrs. Schankweiler bought the neighbors' property and moved from Florida to the house nearby us, a pasture away from the children and me, so they could help us recover from the nightmare. Later, my sister-in-law and her family also moved from Florida to Tennessee so they could assist.

The compassion of the Schankweiler family was astounding. They retired from the church where they had lived and served for thirty years, left their community, traveled to Tennessee, and bought the house right next door to us—all in a matter of weeks. Even those members of the family I did not see often were incredibly supportive. Certainly, everyone was saddened by the events that took Tommy's life, but each member of the Schankweiler family was positive, comforting, and encouraging to the kids and me.

∞§∞

Pap drove me to Chattanooga for my first visit with Bubba where he was incarcerated until the judge weighed in on his future. It was about a three-hour drive from our home in Lawrenceburg, and I appreciated Pap's company. More than that, his spiritual presence comforted me and gave me confidence as I stepped inside to see my seventeen-year-old son. After clearing security, we walked through the heavily barred entrance and into the visitors' room. The large gray automated doors whisked shut and locked behind us. Guards and cameras were positioned at various places in the room. We were guided to a waiting area and instructed to remain there until the officers brought Bubba to us. We were not permitted to go to him.

Still dressed in an orange prison jumpsuit, Bubba was escorted to a cubicle with thick glass separating us and him. We were allowed to sit opposite him and speak to each other through the small speaker hole in the glass. We could see and hear each other well but could not touch. Bubba appeared to be in good health. He didn't seem distraught, anxious about coming home, or emotionally upset. He appeared physically okay, and I was glad he was at least eating and not starving himself in despair. He didn't seem afraid or stressed about how soon the attorney could get him released. Overall, he seemed subdued, calm, and relaxed, almost too quiet.

After greeting each other, I said, "You know you're going to be in here for at least thirty days."

"Yes, I know," he said.

"The lawyer is fighting to get you out as soon as possible, but this is part of the process. You have to be here for evaluation."

"Yeah, I know," he said. Beginning early each morning, Bubba was in counseling sessions all day, grilled by a battery of psychologists. He later told me he never wanted to go to counseling again for the rest of his life.

Then we began talking about the events of Good Friday.

It was during this visit that Bubba told me, "I saw you when Dad was chasing me on the motorcycle."

"What?" I was baffled because I had been searching with all my might hoping to spot Bubba, but I certainly had not. Better yet, Tommy had not seen Bubba. Yet Bubba had seen *us*. It was as though God was protecting him, shielding him from sight in broad daylight.

Bubba said, "I was so tired of running by then, I had started walking. But then I heard Dad's motorcycle fire up, so I started running again. I was tired, ready to die, and figured if he got me, he got me, but I couldn't go any further."

Then Bubba asked me an astounding question. "Mom, when you came past me, why didn't you stop?"

"Stop when? Where?"

"Dad came speeding past me on his motorcycle, and you were right behind him. So why didn't you stop?"

"I never saw you, Bubba," I said.

"Dad turned around at the end of the road, and you were still right behind him. I saw you both times. But you didn't stop."

"Bubba, I did not see you," I said in amazement. I knew there were no bushes or trees close to the road, only pastures. How could I not have seen him?

"Dad looked right at me and went speeding by, and you were right behind him. You even looked at me, Mom, but you never stopped."

"Son, I didn't stop because you weren't there. I was looking for you."

"Mom, you looked right at me," Bubba said.

I got chills as he told me. *How could he know what Tommy did and what I did if he didn't see us?* I thought. Nobody had informed him about that aspect of the day. We hadn't talked about it at the police station. This was our first conversation since those events. He'd had no place to hide along that road, yet I did not see him. More importantly, Tommy had passed right by and looked at Bubba, but didn't see him. I could only conclude that Bubba had been protected by God or an angel. It had been a miracle.

Bubba, Pap, and I talked further, and all too soon, our thirty-minute visitation time evaporated. Pap and I prayed for Bubba, and part of my prayer for him was that any spirit of evil in his life would be broken. I prayed the Lord would renew his heart and mind, and I fought back tears as my son was escorted by the guard out of the room, shuffling along the way because his feet were hooked together with chains and his hands were handcuffed.

During each future visit, I tried to remain composed for Bubba's sake, but my heart broke again each time I saw him in those circumstances. The subsequent visits were much the same as the first; Pap and I were permitted to sit across from Bubba, separated by the thick glass, and talk together for twenty to thirty minutes. That was all.

The uncertainty was heartrending. I still didn't know when or even *if* Bubba would ever be released.

CHAPTER 34

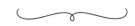

From Nightmares to
Answered Prayers

*E*ven though I knew my husband, Tommy, was dead, he continued to stalk me in my dreams. I could feel his fists pummeling me and his strong hands around my throat. I could hear his voice threatening me and his loud screams echoing through the chambers of my mind as I tried to sleep. Many nights I awakened soaking wet with perspiration, shaking with fear. I prayed the Lord would protect me, and that any spiritual chains of bondage under which the kids and I had been living would be broken. I prayed that God would renew our hearts and minds. Counseling with a therapist, coupled with my faith in God, helped me greatly.

From the first night Bubba was incarcerated, I was never certain he was going to come home. I now recognized it was possible he might go to prison—for a long time. That was hard for me to fathom, knowing what I did about the day of the shooting and the eighteen years of abuse and tyranny Tommy had put us through. But despite the evidence and history of abuse all over our property, Bubba had pulled the trigger. There was no guarantee that a judge—or a possible jury—would fully understand why or how our family had gotten to that point.

Week after week I met with our attorney, but he didn't give me a lot of hope. I kept waiting for him to say that everything was going to be okay, but he never would. He refused to sugarcoat the situation or offer false hope that Bubba could easily elude prison. Instead, he often implied that Bubba's case could go either way, and I needed to be prepared for that.

He carefully walked me back through the events of Good Friday—painstakingly searching for any small detail that I may have missed that might make a difference in Bubba's defense.

Meanwhile, the folks from Lawrenceburg stuck with our family. Many wrote letters of encouragement to Bubba. Several of his high school teachers spoke to television and newspaper reporters, telling them what a great kid Bubba was. The community rallied around him, writing letters in support of him and signing petitions to the judge expressing the opinion that Bubba's actions were mitigated by the horror of the abuse that had gone on for so long in our home. Almost daily, I received cards and letters encouraging our family. I received so many cards I strung them all together and hung them around the perimeter of our house, starting in the kitchen, then stretching down the hallway and into the living room. Looking around the interior of the house each day, the kids and I could see abundant and surprising evidence of the love and support from our community.

I kept the kids home from school for the first few weeks following the incident, so one of their teachers called and asked if our kids could come to the school to receive some gifts and hand-made cards from their classmates and teachers. "Sure," I said. "I think they would love to do that. We'll look forward to seeing you."

When the group gathered at the school, they showered Timothy, Tonie Jo, and Tayler with cards, stuffed animals, Bibles, and lots of hugs. The kids responded enthusiastically, and I could tell it was a good experience for them. Not only did they sense they were loved and accepted by their teachers and peers at school, but they also understood that they had done nothing wrong regarding their dad's actions.

⁂

Near the end of May, my attorney called me. "Can you come to my office as soon as possible?" he asked. His voice sounded strained. "I have some news, and I'd like to talk with you about our options."

I had no idea what he meant, but I responded, "Yes. I'll be right there." I couldn't get to his office fast enough.

Daniel Freeman greeted me in his usual manner, calm and undemonstrative. I sat down in his office and waited for him to explain.

He spoke ponderously, but with a hint of a smile. "It seems that after reviewing the police reports from the investigation and combing through all the evidence at the crime scene, the district attorney has decided not to pursue first-degree murder charges."

That was a relief!

Bubba had initially been charged with first-degree murder for shooting his dad; now the district attorney was offering a plea agreement that would reduce the charges. "The DA is willing to give your son a post-plea diversion on a no-contest plea to voluntary manslaughter." Daniel Freeman continued, "If the judge agrees with this," he shook some papers in his hand, "Tommy would only have to serve a maximum of five years."

My heart leaped into my throat. *Five years?*

Attorney Freeman must have sensed my apprehension. He continued, "Yes, five years' probation."

"Probation?" I asked. "No prison time?"

233

"No, none."

Mr. Freeman explained that prior to Patsy cleaning up the crime scene, the investigation discovered so much evidence throughout the house and yard that proved we were in a deadly struggle on Good Friday and feared for our lives. Pictures from inside our house showed broken windows and smashed doorframes, with bloodstains spattered on the walls and floors. They also noted that Tommy had bolted all the windows in our living room shut. He had put large wooden shutters over the windows and then screwed them closed so they could not be opened.

Of course, the police also found pictures that were strategically hung on our walls to cover bullet holes or places where Tommy had punched through the drywall. They also noted the bullet holes sprayed in the concrete driveway and other random bullet holes inside the house. They discovered Tommy's arsenal of guns—some sitting openly in each room, others he concealed, and the guns Tommy had hidden above the ceiling tiles.

The authorities found the framing square Tommy had hurled at Bubba, and the stainless steel pan with the large dent that Bubba had used to defend himself. They also found the nearly empty fifth of whiskey Tommy had last been drinking, located precisely where I told the police I had seen it. The bottle had been full earlier that morning. And they found the single spent .22 caliber bullet casing.

Mr. Freeman somberly said, "The evidence spoke louder than any of your voices."

He explained to me the investigators concluded that when Bubba returned that fateful day, he fully expected to find his father in a drunken sleep, or begging for our forgiveness, as he had done so many times previously. Bubba quickly assessed the situation and made the difficult decision to end the violence before his dad came after him and the rest of us.

"The house gave up its secrets, the investigators concluded, and told the story. No jury would convict Bubba for choosing to protect himself and you that day," the attorney said.

For a moment I thought a smile may have crossed Daniel Freeman's face, but he quickly regained his composure. "The post-plea diversion," he said, "does demand five years of strict probation, during which Bubba will have to report regularly to a probation officer and abide by all the other rules regarding probation in our state. Assuming Bubba will have no further incidents, he will be totally free in five years."

There was a risk involved with accepting this plea. Bubba's case would be moved from juvenile court to adult court. But the attorney seemed hopeful that the judge would consider the mitigating circumstances, including statements by the neighbors that "there was always something going on at that house."

Mr. Freeman had invited me to his office to discuss our options. But what options did we need to discuss?

"No prison time" was all I needed to hear. I suddenly felt as though a hundred-pound weight had been lifted off my heart. I took a deep breath and allowed myself to relax for the first time in weeks. When I stood up to leave Attorney Freeman's office, I felt lighter, as though I was walking on the air. This was the news I had been hoping and praying to hear. The judge still had to agree to the plan, but Mr. Freeman for once felt confident that she would.

"Yes!" I said. "We will accept that plea and the change from juvenile court to adult court." The attorney attempted to explain some of the details I didn't understand, but I understood enough. It was possible, if not highly likely, that Bubba could be coming home to us. As I turned to leave, Mr. Freeman called, "Sandee Jo, this is the first time I've seen you smile since we met."

I hadn't been aware I was smiling, but I'm sure I couldn't help it either.

I went out to my car and, for several minutes, simply sat there and cried. Finally, I turned on the ignition, and when the motor started, so did my car's CD player. Nicole C. Mullen's crystal clear voice filled the car: "When I call on Jesus, all things are possible." Drawing from Isaiah 40, the lyrics continued, "I can mount on wings like eagles and soar."

I felt God was using Nicole to remind me that He was bigger than all of the obstacles we faced, and that somehow, Jesus would bring us through. I sat there listening and weeping. But now the tears were different. I felt God saying, "It's going to be okay." My hope was renewed that I would see my son again, free and thriving.

The song "Call On Jesus" by Nicole C. Mullen had been my anchor for a long time, but now it possessed even more meaning. I had called on Jesus again and again about Bubba's situation, and God had communicated to me through the words of that song, giving me the reassurance I needed. Tears rolled down my face as the words and music wrapped around my heart and mind like a warm, soothing blanket. The overwhelming comfort that settled in the car that day came straight from heaven. Although I understood there were still legal hurdles to overcome, I had complete confidence that Bubba would be home with our family soon.

CHAPTER 35

Project Fresh Start

Shortly after news of the shooting became public, one of Tommy's former classmates called James Crocker in Florida to inform him of Tommy's death. James made some phone calls to get more information, but nobody could tell him how Tommy had died. James still had Tommy's phone number, so he dialed it.

My mom, who was still staying with us, answered Tommy's phone when it rang.

"Hi, um, my name is James Crocker," James began uneasily.

Although she hadn't seen him in nearly twenty years, Mom remembered James from Tommy's and my wedding. After some brief formalities, James mustered the boldness to ask, "How did Tommy die?"

"Oh, you haven't heard?" my mom asked him.

"No, I haven't," James replied.

Mom didn't even try to be vague or tactful. She bluntly said, "Well, the oldest son shot him. Bubba shot him." She explained that Tommy had been extremely violent, and that Bubba had taken all he could stand.

Following their conversation, James did an Internet search and found the news stories online. From there, he called Pastor Schankweiler to express his condolences and learn more about the family's plans for a memorial service in Florida.

James and his wife, Marcy, and their three-year-old adopted daughter, Charlee, attended the service in Florida. James approached me at the dinner hosted by the church following the funeral service. "I'm so sorry for your loss," James said sincerely. I thanked him and we spoke briefly, barely a minute or two. I didn't really know James, but I remembered him as one of the groomsmen from our wedding, and as one of the "kidnappers" who had blindfolded me at the wedding reception. I also knew of his call to Tommy less than a month or so earlier, inviting him to their class reunion—and Tommy's adamant refusal to attend.

Although I was unaware of it, before leaving the church that day, James approached Pastor Schankweiler about how to best help the grieving family.

"Well, I've been up there," Pastor Schankweiler replied, "and the house needs a lot of work. It's in pretty bad shape. A number of windows are broken out, doors broken, you know." The pastor did not mention the bullet holes in the driveway or the various spots in the walls where his son had punched or shot holes in the plasterboard. I later learned that the authorities investigating Tommy's death had discovered more than forty bullet holes in our home.

"Oh my," James said, shaking his head sadly.

"Yes, they were trying to do a little remodeling downstairs before…" The pastor's voice broke off, and tears filled his eyes.

James nodded. "Thank you, Pastor," he said. "We'll figure something out."

Later, James talked to his wife and said, "Let's plan a trip up there and see if we can help my buddy's family."

The Crockers did not have my phone number, nor did Pastor Schankweiler volunteer it, but a few weeks later, they showed up out of the blue in Tennessee. Apparently, they had kept in contact with Pastor Schankweiler, but their visit was a surprise to me. Pap showed them around and reminded James about the work on the basement that still needed done, the same project on which Tommy, Timmy, and Bubba had been working when Bubba had cut the board incorrectly.

Looking back, I suppose I should have been embarrassed by the appearance of our home, with all the broken and boarded-up windows and the pockmarks in the walls. There were sections of half-done plasterboard where Tommy had begun to put up drywall and never finished. The ceilings in the girls' sleeping areas, where Tonie Jo slept on a makeshift bed on the concrete floor, were unfinished as well. Outside the house was another incomplete project of Tommy's: the half-built wall. Everywhere I looked, there was so much clutter and dishevelment. But I was still in survival mode, so I let Pap guide James on a tour of the house.

When Pap informed James that I planned to keep the house and continue living there with the kids, James got an idea. He felt compelled to help renovate the entire home where Tommy's death had taken place.

James loved the television show *Extreme Makeover: Home Edition*, starring Ty Pennington. James said aloud to himself, "I feel like this family needs an extreme home makeover." The couple even contacted the television show, hoping to pique the producers' interest, but they ran into too many roadblocks and requests for personal and financial information they could not readily provide—not to mention the extended time it might take to get the project slated on the show's schedule. So James and Marcy dreamed up their own idea of renovating our home as an extreme makeover—the self-funded, small, country-town version.

As Pap and James discussed the possibilities, I caught bits and pieces of their conversation: "We might need to knock out all but three load-bearing walls upstairs, and all the walls downstairs…"

I heard them debating ideas, but to be honest, most of the comments didn't really register in my mind. It was certainly unusual to have relative strangers show up at our house and begin suggesting we "knock it down and start over," so at one point I asked James, "Are you a building contractor?"

"Oh no," he said with a laugh. "Not me. I'm in the manufacturing business."

I later learned they didn't even have a blueprint. But I trusted Pap, and I remembered the phone call from James in mid-February. Following their conversation, Tommy had told me James had become quite successful, and that I should have married someone like him. Knowing our little house needed a lot of work and that I had no funds to finance it, I felt that allowing James and Pap to move forward with some of their ideas seemed worth the risk.

Similar to the television program *Extreme Makeover: Home Edition*, the generous couple thought it would enhance the challenge to commit their volunteer construction team, which was still unrecruited, to complete the work in only six days! They believed volunteers would be motivated by the seemingly impossible deadline. James recruited two videographers to document the work for our family and other interested viewers.

The Crockers also came up with the name "Project Fresh Start." They said, "This family needs a change of scenery, a fresh start." To begin enlisting help, James asked Pap, "Who is the most influential man in Deerfield Baptist Church, where the family attends?"

"Well, probably Bill Dixon," Pap said.

James found Bill Dixon, dressed in his overalls and suspenders, standing in front of a grain silo on the farm where he and my friend,

Gail, lived, just a mile or two up the road from our home on Piney Road. The quintessential friendly, hardworking farmer, Bill always seemed to have time for conversation, and James quickly captured his attention when he began talking about helping our family. Helping others is what Bill and Gail's lives are all about. James briefly described the project they had in mind and the need for securing building permits and subcontractors. James asked, "Bill, when you think about contractors in this area, who are the best of the best? Who has the best reputation and the most influence?"

"That would probably be Richardson Builders in Lawrenceburg," Bill said. "The owner is Steve Wright."

That's all James needed to hear. He didn't know Steve Wright, but he called him and asked, "Steve, would you have time for coffee?"

Steve responded positively, so he and James got together at a gas station convenience store. Only then did James reveal the purpose for their meeting. "We want to give the Schankweiler family a fresh start," he said. "But it's hard to start anew when you see holes in the walls everywhere and doors and glass broken out. I'd like to recruit a crew that can not only fix the mess, but also make the home much better and more inviting for the family."

Word had gotten around the small town of Lawrenceburg by then, and most people knew about what had happened at our house. The incident had been reported on all the television stations and in the newspapers as far away as Nashville, so the locals knew some of the horrific details. James got down to business. He asked, "Steve, I'm wondering if you'd consider donating some of your time and expertise to executing our own version of an extreme home makeover, right here on Piney Road."

Steve did not even hesitate. He volunteered to help, so James peppered him with questions: "Who is the best drywall contractor around? Who's the best painter? The best window man? Who's the best carpenter? The best electrician?"

Steve gave James the names of several subcontractors, and James was on his way again. He met with Megan and Trevor Hamby, who also attended church with our family and owned Hamby Electric Company. They agreed to help. Trevor's dad, Kenny Hamby, offered to head up the framing crew, along with his son, Seth.

Next, James had a similar conversation with a local painter, Scott Fincher. Scott and his two daughters, Maggie and Brianna, brimmed with excitement over the opportunity for the Fincher paint crew to do the painting on the proposed renovation project.

A "country snowball effect" started rolling. Tennessee is known as the Volunteer State, and James quickly discovered that the nickname was appropriate. Roger Emmerson volunteered to do the air-conditioning and heating work on the house, and Summertown Metals offered to supply the metal roofing. Happy and J.C. Wisdom would haul stone for the driveway, while local landscaping artists Randy Alley and Marty Manning would donate trees, shrubs, sod, mulch, and flowers, plus the labor to install them.

Before long, James had recruited a small army of volunteers willing to help renovate the home where Bubba had shot Tommy. In fact, nearly everyone James talked with was willing to help.

When James couldn't locate a local drywall expert, he called his friend Steve Addison, who owned Addison Drywall in Florida. Steve agreed to supply his best team and finishing crew to do the job with excellence. James found a plumber in Pennsylvania, Gary Gattone, who offered his services. Another guy out of Ohio had a big RV company, and he donated some money. In all, James recruited skilled workers from nine separate states and convinced them to travel at their own expense to help renovate our home in Tennessee. His own brother Jeff, a roofer in Ohio, volunteered and offered to bring his wife and daughters to help with the home decorations. Friends from Florida, including Paul Davis, a gentleman who had no personal connection to the Schankweiler family, came on board to install a fabulous new kitchen. In only two days, at least eleven contractors committed their resources and promised to help on the project. Many of the contractors and workers James recruited did not know anything about our situation, other than a horrible tragedy had taken place. That so many good-hearted people would commit to Project Fresh Start was a tribute to the tenacity of James's recruiting efforts, but even more so to the kindness, compassion, and goodness of God, inspiring folks to get involved in whatever ways they could help.

Once James had the construction leaders lined up, he and his wife hosted a volunteer dinner at a local restaurant the following evening. Pastor Tony Gordy, still relatively new to our church as the pastor, attended and promised to do his best to galvanize the church family in support of Project Fresh Start.

When James and his family returned to Florida, he contacted radio stations to publicize the effort; he designed a website, projectfreshstart.com, and announced the vision that the volunteers planned to gut the house and renovate it. His cousin Britton Winter drew the floor plan, and the local Lawrenceburg high school drafting class came to our home and did all the measurements. Together, James and Britton developed the idea of knocking a forty-foot hole in the back wall and putting a five-hundred-square-foot addition onto the house, including a big kitchen and a living area with a cathedral ceiling. That required the removal of a portion of our existing roof and the addition of new trusses to carry the load. They also decided to replace the entire electrical system in the house, including the air-conditioning unit.

The volunteers developed a plan to construct four bedrooms for the kids downstairs, as well as two bathrooms—one for the girls and one for the boys. Adding the bathrooms meant sinking large holes in the cement slab that formed our basement floor and installing sewage sump pumps to eliminate the waste. James returned in May to work on that. While he was there, two of his friends, Todd and Liz Carson, made the initial large donation of $20,000 to begin funding the project. Their generous contribution was the first of many that Project Fresh Start would receive.

Since there was room for only one window in the basement, the volunteers decided to give that room to Tonie Jo. It had been her horse that Tommy shot with a twelve-gauge shotgun. So they designed her room to include the window so she could look outside and see her horse—a *new* horse Steve Wright had found for sale and had purchased for her.

Marcy took on the responsibilities of decorating the kids' rooms, and she was so creative. She worked hard to make every detail special for the kids and me. She sent magazines to the kids and asked them to browse through them—then when they saw a decoration they liked, a color, or any kind of furnishing that appealed to them, they were to cut out the photo, glue it to a piece of cardboard, then mail the boards back to Marcy. She called several times and spoke to each of the kids to learn about their personalities, their favorite colors, and their tastes, to which she then tried to match the decorations and furnishings. She wanted the kids to enjoy bedrooms that reflected their own interests.

Although I was focused on Bubba during the planning and preparation of the home renovation, I was often overwhelmed with emotion by it all. I was amazed that people we didn't even know would care so much to help us in such generous and self-effacing ways.

James and I had some brief communication, but most of my phone conversations about the needs at the house were with Marcy. She would tell me, "Okay, make sure the decoration boards are back to me by this date." I'd remind the kids, "Hey, pick out the stuff you like because we gotta get the pictures in the mail."

By now, I had returned to work at the rehabilitation center, so I had a lot going on. But in truth, I had no idea how big of a job the renovation would be. I didn't fully comprehend that James had put together a team of plumbers, electricians, drywall installers, roofers, and others—all volunteers—to remodel our entire home. In six days!

CHAPTER 36

Released

As Attorney Freeman had indicated, when all the legal machinations were complete, the judge ruled on Bubba's case under a nolo contendere plea of voluntary manslaughter, with a final charge of a post-plea diversion. That became the basis on which Bubba was to be released, as well as a five-year probationary period. The judge went even further, granting that after five years of good behavior, the incident could be expunged from Bubba's record. That was especially good news because Bubba wanted to enlist in the military after high school.

Our entire family was so excited to finally learn the judge's ruling. Pap and I wasted no time, and the moment we received the word, we drove to Chattanooga to bring Bubba home. I took him a fresh change of clothes so he could cast off the orange prison garb. Pap and I arrived and went immediately into the office, where I signed some forms since Bubba was still a minor.

Then we walked out, and Bubba was suddenly free—at least free from the constraints of incarceration. It would be a long, slow process before he was truly free from all he had experienced.

Interestingly, James Crocker had returned to Tennessee and was back checking on renovation details at our house the day Bubba was released. I appreciated that James had driven all the way from Florida to Tennessee to do advance preparation for Project Fresh Start, so I certainly didn't want to be rude to him. On the other hand, I worried about having a relative stranger with us when Bubba first returned home.

Even though it had been several weeks since the shooting, I knew it would be extremely difficult for Bubba to step back inside our house—even more so to pass by Tommy's and my former bedroom, or the basement where the last battle had begun. There was no way I could prepare him for that. All I could do was pray for God's Spirit to protect his heart and mind.

Bubba was rather subdued during the drive home from Chattanooga with Pap and me. The three of us were thrilled by the judge's decision, and we talked briefly about that—but for most of the three-hour trip, each of us remained relatively quiet. I looked out the window and mulled over what the future might hold, but I was more concerned about the immediate situation Bubba would face back at home. At last, Pap pulled our car down Piney Road and came to a stop in our driveway. Bubba stoically got out of the vehicle and walked directly into the house without a moment of hesitation. Pap and I followed him to provide support if Bubba needed it.

He didn't.

He seemed to process the scene with remarkable calmness and serenity. He saw James working on something at the house, and the two exchanged brief hellos but not much more. As Bubba continued into the interior of our home, I stood back a bit, allowing him to silently absorb it all.

In the days ahead, our family would attend counseling sessions with a Christian therapist in Lawrenceburg. Those sessions helped us move forward rather than sink back into painful memories. Bubba accompanied us to a few sessions, but then he said, "Mom, I don't want to go back to any more counseling. I had so many sessions in Chattanooga, I need a break."

I understood that, but the younger children and I continued to go to counseling sessions for months following the incident.

Fortunately, we were only at the house a few weeks before Project Fresh Start captured our attention.

It had been years since I had slept peacefully through the night, without fearing that Tommy would get up and start another rampage. Now I awakened each day to a life relatively free from worry. I discovered freedoms that I had not experienced in eighteen years—simple things such as lingering in the grocery store long enough to talk with someone without fearing that Tommy would grill me inquisition-style when I returned home. I went out to eat occasionally, went shopping, and formed new friendships. I realized that my opinion mattered, and even if someone disagreed with me or I with them, that was okay. I relearned how to make decisions for myself and for my family. I rediscovered how much I enjoyed wearing clothes that I liked. Rather than acquiescing to Tommy's dictatorial desires or choices, I discovered that I could choose for myself. I could make mistakes without fear of being excoriated, or worse yet, beaten up physically or emotionally. It was an entirely new life, and I was excited about our family's future.

Strangely, I also had to relearn how to cry. For years the kids and I had forced ourselves to restrain our emotions because our tears only spurred on Tommy's insolence. Even when Tommy spanked the kids, they rarely cried for long. I had learned to subvert my emotions as well. I dared not let Tommy see me cry because I knew my tears would intensify his anger and prolong the beatings. When I did allow myself to weep, I cried in the shower or in the car by myself.

Now it was okay to cry, and I let the tears flow freely. But I also learned to laugh more and worry less. Overall, despite the events that had changed us forever, I was excited about the future. The Lord's steadfast love was new every morning.

The Christian community in Lawrenceburg continued to rally around our family. They were so supportive—praying for us, bringing us food, and making sure we were okay—so I went back to church soon after the memorial services. Church was a safe space for me. Going back to work was more of a challenge. I only felt comfortable going back to work full-time once I knew Bubba was coming home. We needed the income, and I felt ready to go back— but I was unprepared for the reality of walking into the workplace where everyone knew about my family and, more specifically, how Tommy had treated us for years.

I had been working at NHC rehabilitation center prior to the shooting. I worked with postoperative patients who had recently been released from the hospital but were still in need of close monitoring—including medications, IVs, physical therapy, and other treatments. On another hall, we had long-term care patients. I needed to have my head together when I returned.

My administrator was gracious. "Whenever you feel ready to come back, that's fine," she said.

"I think I'm ready," I replied confidently.

"Okay," she said. "Come on back to work."

"Great. But please tell people that I really don't want to talk about anything. If they ask me for any details, I will fall apart."

"I understand," my administrator said. "And I will put out the word."

Of course, despite her best efforts, my colleagues and friends had questions the day I returned to work. With the best of intentions, they asked questions such as, "How are you doing? How are the kids doing?" And the question everyone asked: "How is Bubba doing?"

I did my best to field their questions, but I couldn't make it through the day. By eleven a.m., I went to my administrator and said, "I need to go home."

She hugged me and wisely replied, "That's fine. We'll try it again next week."

We did—shortly before Bubba was released. And I did much better.

CHAPTER 37

A Mountaintop Experience

On Sunday, June 29, the night before Project Fresh Start was to begin, I came home from work to find construction vehicles parked everywhere. Volunteers were lugging tools and equipment all around our house and property, preparing for the next day when the clock would start and the home makeover challenge would begin. A huge white tent stood in our front yard, with a large sign displaying the names of the major sponsors who supported the project, as well as the amount of money they still hoped to raise.

That night, some of the volunteers lingered long enough for James to ask the kids, Granny, Pap, and me to join them on the back patio. I was not familiar with James Crocker's sense of humor, so I was stunned when I heard him say, "Sandee Jo, we're short on help and..." James paused and looked at our family and the volunteers standing nearby. Then he deadpanned, "We've arranged for you to be off work all week."

I was standing there in my nursing uniform, having just gotten off work. Furthermore, I'd been off work for two months and had just gone back to nursing. I knew I couldn't take time off again so soon. As James talked, I thought, *There's no way.*

But James continued, saying, "We're really concerned about getting everything done. And we know how important this is for your family."

I stared back at James, thinking that at any moment he would explain how the kids and I would possibly be able to help renovate the house for the next six days.

But James surprised me. He said, "Sandee Jo, instead of helping with the house, we've arranged for you and the kids to go to Gatlinburg to enjoy a big, beautiful log cabin on top of the mountain—all expenses paid. We have tickets for you to go to Dollywood, Dolly Parton's theme park, and other attractions. You'll have a car at your service waiting for you there. And you're leaving tomorrow!"

The group on the porch cheered and crowed loudly, as the kids and I looked at each other in disbelief.

It all sounded fantastic, but I was perplexed as I listened, wondering how to tell James that I couldn't possibly accept his generous offer because I *had* to go to work. The administrators and staff at the rehab center had been so kind and accommodating to me since Tommy's death, allowing me to have nearly two months of administrative leave. I had just returned to work and couldn't possibly ask for another six days off.

James was still talking as I was fretting. "And don't worry, Sandee Jo. We have already contacted your administrators, who have graciously made arrangements for you to be off work this whole next week. And some donors have contributed funds so you won't miss a day's pay."

What? I couldn't believe it. How had he pulled this off without anyone at work telling me? James had left no stone unturned. I felt as though I was dreaming. *The kids and I are leaving for Gatlinburg—tomorrow!*

The next day, more than a hundred people were in our yard, all wearing hard hats and ready for Project Fresh Start to commence—but not before they saw us off in style. The kids and I stood in front of our house as James made a few announcements. Moments later, a full-sized white limousine pulled into our driveway. It had come to pick us up! None of us had ever seen inside a limousine, much less ridden in one. The volunteers smiled broadly as the chauffeur opened the back doors for us and the kids and I climbed inside the huge vehicle, overwhelmed and in awe. The workers all threw their hard hats up in the air as we pulled out of the driveway and down the lane. We were all tremendously excited and ready for some fun; but even more, we were ready to get away from the memories of home and enjoy time in God's creation.

It was a special blessing that Bubba had been released from custody in time to accompany us on the trip. So we were on our way to the Great Smoky Mountains—in a limo! And Bubba was coming with us! James or Marcy could not possibly have known the timing of Bubba's release, but God did!

The limousine stopped at Bubba's probation office so I could get the paperwork permitting Bubba to leave town. Initially, the judge had ruled that he was to stay in the county, but when she learned about the incredible plans of Project Fresh Start, she granted Bubba permission. He could accompany us to the mountains, though he would not be fully cleared for other travel until much later.

I'm sure we made for an odd sight pulling up to the probation office in a limousine.

⳧⳨

Back at our house, the demolition and remodeling process was already well underway. More than 130 volunteers feverishly worked together with hammers thudding and saws buzzing. Each team of volunteers was assembled with a project manager who knew the plan and how to coordinate the work of carpenters, electricians, plumbers, drywall installers, tile layers, and more—all at the same time!

Steve Wright was later heard to say, "James Crocker was just the man for the job." When asked why, Steve quipped, "James knows little to nothing about construction. Anyone who knows construction knows you cannot schedule workers to lay tile on the floor in the same bathroom where plumbers are installing a tub and shower!" It was a funny comment, especially since James had admitted early on that he was not a contractor.

While the construction team was busy tearing down and rebuilding portions of our house, Marcy and another team picked up supplies, furniture, and decorations. Yet another team purchased food and did all the cooking for the volunteers. They provided breakfast, lunch, and dinner under the big white circus tent every day so the construction team would not have to leave the property. Some volunteers brought their own campers and stayed on our land so they could work longer hours. Many people took vacation time from work so they could participate in Project Fresh Start. Even the local sheriff—the same authorities who had arrested Bubba—made an appearance to assure people of their support for the community project.

About eighty of the volunteers attended Deerfield Baptist Church and other local churches. They were such good people, and they worked so hard. Everything they needed was provided. That was a testimony itself.

By that time, Pap and Granny had purchased the property next door, so they offered their barn as a work area where the volunteers could assemble cabinets and other items before transferring them to our home.

The crew gathered and worked feverishly each day from June 30 through July 5, in the intense heat of the Tennessee summer.

Businesses and individuals from the community also donated food for the workers.

Pastor Schankweiler volunteered and worked diligently to pour a new cement sidewalk. He was one of the last to quit working each day. The volunteer carpenters redid all the floors in the house, including the kitchen. They refreshed the landscaping in front of the house, put in a new driveway, and added a large wooden deck out back.

Buttermilk Wisdom kept everyone encouraged. "I'm just proud to be here," he said repeatedly.

While the renovation work was being done, the kids and I had no idea what was happening.

The trip to the Gatlinburg area took about three hours, and the kids and I were mesmerized the entire way, staring out the windows of the limousine as the fancy car whisked us across Tennessee. When we approached our cabin, the limo slowly wound around each hairpin curve, climbing higher and higher up the mountain-side to the very top. Finally, the limo stopped in front of a cabin perched on the pinnacle of the mountain, and we all jumped out and took in the view of the magnificent scenery surrounding us. It was a panorama of beauty. In every direction we gazed, the majesty of God was on full display.

We stepped inside the cabin to look around and were once again awestruck. The cabin that would be our home for the next six days was three stories high—on top of the mountain! The kitchen had been stocked with all of our favorite foods, including plenty of fun snacks—the sorts of "luxuries" we could never afford because Tommy usually spent any discretionary income on booze. Here the kids discovered more treats than they could possibly eat! No detail was missed.

The views from every room were incredible, and each of us had our own bedroom. There was also a game room that the kids found right away. But the real surprise was the large balcony that jutted out from the cabin and faced the picturesque mountains and valleys. It was surrounded by swaying trees and chirping birds and lined with rocking chairs. At the far end of the porch was a large heated jacuzzi. The entire place was truly spectacular, and I continually felt my emotions overwhelming me as I thought of the kindness of so many people who had made this experience possible for us. In a real way, it was the first time our family had ever been on a vacation that didn't revolve around Tommy's hunting or fishing plans. Tayler kept saying, "I've never been in a cabin before," in her cute Tennessee drawl.

That night, I fell asleep to the sweet smell of cedar and the warm comfort of knowing that all of my children were safe and under the same roof. We were already having an unbelievable experience, and we'd only just begun. My heart was full, and I thanked the Lord for His amazing love.

For the next six days, the kids and I took in Gatlinburg's main attractions. We enjoyed an entire day at Dollywood, where we rode fabulous roller coasters, heard great music, and ate delicious food. Another day, we visited the WonderWorks park and Ripley's Believe It or Not! We went horseback riding in the mountains, ice-skating, and roller-skating. The boys even managed to do a little fishing in the crystal clear rippling mountain streams. We ate at the most popular places, and at the end of each day, we ambled back to the cabin physically tired from another day of fresh experiences. We were the quintessential tourists, but we didn't care! We laughed together and simply had fun.

I loved hearing the kids' constant chatter and healthy noise. The happy commotion kept my mind busy. But when everyone went to sleep, the quiet surrounded me and pressed in on me. I prayed that the nightmares would not torment my sleep. They had been happening often since Tommy's death, and at times, they seemed painfully real. I'd see him in my dreams, looming over me by my bed, bent over and screaming in my face with his fists clenched. He told me I could never run away from him, and that Bubba had made a big mistake. Now, Tommy threatened in my nightmares, he was going to make us all suffer more than ever before.

I woke up terrified and trembling, afraid to close my eyes again lest I fall back asleep. I had not yet learned to take spiritual authority over such nightmares, but I recognized these visions were not from God. I prayed for Jesus and His angels to protect the kids and me, and especially to guard our minds.

At one point during the week, the kids and I paused long enough to have some family photos taken at the cabin. That, too, was a gift from Project Fresh Start. The team sent a cameraman to capture some great photos and videos of the kids there. Although we didn't know it at the time, a number of those photos would show up again in a few days.

I took another break from our family fun activities to accept an interview request while we were at the cabin. A reporter drove over from Nashville and asked me to share some of the details about what had happened on Good Friday and how our family had been dealing with it. I had not done an interview about the incident aside from the police interrogations, but now that Bubba was back with us, I was more willing to talk about what we had experienced.

The story landed on the front page of the *Tennessean*, Nashville's leading newspaper, associated with *USA Today*. Suddenly, our story was everywhere, and I understood for the first time the potential

260 IF WALLS COULD TALK

our story had to possibly help others dealing with dysfunctional or abusive relationships. Prior to that moment, I had been so absorbed with survival, coping with our own pain and recovery, that it hadn't really occurred to me that other people might be interested in or helped in some way by our negative *and* positive experiences. I recognized that despite the difficulties, our story was one of hope and survival that needed to be shared. I decided to accept interview requests if they came...and they did.

For the time being, though, I was content to enjoy this special time with my children. The mountains were beautiful, and I was with the ones I loved most—so even though I knew we had to face reality when we got home, and work through our emotional baggage, I was grateful for this opportunity to simply relax and be ourselves.

Several times during the week, as we lounged in the jacuzzi, the kids and I talked about what we imagined our home would look like when we returned. We really had no clue what was happening there aside from the conversations we'd had with Marcy. We had dreams, of course, since we had shared our wish lists with her. The kids were excited to see their bedrooms, and I was excited to see the kitchen. Regardless, it was exhilarating to know that when this glorious vacation was over, we still had our "new" home to look forward to enjoying.

CHAPTER 38

Move That Tractor!

On Saturday, July 6, 2008, we packed our clothes and piled into the same long white limousine for our trip home. We felt renewed. We had enjoyed a fabulous and refreshing vacation, but we were nonetheless excited about heading back across Tennessee to Lawrenceburg. None of the kids mentioned the bad memories associated with the house we had left behind—only their anticipation of their new bedrooms.

After several hours, the driver pulled the limo into the parking lot in front of Self's Market, just a short distance from our home. There, the Project Fresh Start volunteers had arranged for a cameraman to meet us and record our arrival. The cameraman climbed in the limo with us, and as the white limousine approached our driveway, he asked, "What do you think?"

I'm not sure I answered his question. I was too overwhelmed by the sight that met my eyes. People cheered and waved as the car rolled over the freshly laid gravel leading to our house. The expressions on the faces of the volunteers said it all. They had worked all week long to renovate our house and property, and their exhaustion had turned to exuberance that they had accomplished their goal.

The limousine stopped in the driveway and was immediately surrounded by dozens of friends, both old and new. The Crockers and Pap were at the front of the crowd. Inside the limo, my four children and I excitedly peered out the windows. When we stepped out of the vehicle, everyone applauded and cheered as though we were important celebrities. A reporter and another cameraman stood nearby, chronicling the event. It was a marvelous experience to receive the outpouring of love from people—some of whom we had never met—who simply wanted us to know our lives mattered to God and to them. We had never been the objects of such attention in our lives!

On the Friday night before our homecoming party, the volunteers had asked our family friend Buttermilk Wisdom to park his tractor in front of the house so we couldn't fully see the house when we first pulled down our lane. The idea was to prolong the excitement, similar to how *Extreme Makeover: Home Edition* used a large bus to block the view of the completed project.

James and Marcy greeted us as soon as we got out of the limo. Friends ushered us to the center of the crowd, where James spoke into a microphone. He welcomed us home and recognized the great team of heroes who had donated their time, skills, and money to Project Fresh Start. Meanwhile, the kids and I stood facing the car with our backs to the house so we couldn't see it yet.

James concluded his remarks, and then, just as family and friends did on the *Extreme Makeover* television episodes, everyone began to chant. But instead of saying, "Somebody move that bus!" the line of people began calling out, "Move that tractor! Move that *tractor!*"

People in front of the tractor continued cheering and calling out in unison, "*Buttermilk! Move that tractor!*" The kids and I joyfully joined in calling out, "Buttermilk, move that tractor!" Everyone was smiling, laughing, shouting, and applauding. What a scene!

Buttermilk cranked the motor and slowly pulled the tractor away from the front of the house to the applause and loud cheers from the crowd. When the kids and I turned around...we were shocked! There was our house, but it didn't look the same as when we had pulled out of our driveway six days earlier. It looked fresh and new! Sure enough, somebody called out, "This is your new house!" and the crowd erupted in cheers again.

I was overwhelmed with emotion as the kids and I walked through the front door of the house. There were no bullet holes, no gaping holes in the walls—none of that. It looked brand-new! Instead of the pictures I had strategically placed to cover wall damage, there were now beautiful framed photos of the kids and me in the mountains. The volunteers had enlarged the photos the cameraman had taken at the cabin earlier in the week, and now they decorated our new home, commemorating our fresh start.

As I gazed around the living room in awe, it struck me how radical the transformation was. I was speechless. Our living room looked like a photograph from a magazine. From the living room I could see into the kitchen and dining room, where the ceilings were now high and the entire area was open and spacious. Each room was filled with new furniture, and the walls were freshly painted and tastefully decorated.

Downstairs, where the battle between Tommy and Bubba had begun barely three-and-a-half months earlier, a comfortable living room greeted us at the bottom of the staircase. The space led to four bedrooms, one in each corner of the house. The bedrooms were decorated in the kids' favorite colors and reflected their hobbies and interests.

Tayler's room was all about pink—pink bedding, pink polka dots on the walls, even a pink lampshade. Bubba's room featured duck hunting scenes, with a deer antler lamp and a large quilt depicting ducks. Timothy's room was all about fishing. Marcy had found a wall mural with a fisherman in a stream, so it looked as though Timothy was looking out a window overlooking a creek. Tonie Jo's room had a horse theme. Her bed boasted a big leather headboard, created by a craftsman on the site, that featured large metal inset buttons. Even her lamps were made from cowboy boots. Every detail in the kids' rooms had been carefully and lovingly customized to each child. I was in awe, and my eyes stayed filled with tears of joy and thankfulness as waves of emotion flooded over me.

We not only stepped inside our newly renovated home; we stepped into an entirely different sort of existence. All reminders of the horrors that had taken place there had been removed and replaced by happy pictures.

As nightfall approached, friends and family members continued to celebrate with us. After the kids and I finished touring the house, we opened it up for everyone to walk through. We stood at our front door and greeted each person who came by, thanking them sincerely for their kindnesses to our family.

At seven o'clock, a music group from Nashville played live music for us under the tent. Then we closed out the evening with a "bang," as everyone enjoyed a large display of fireworks above our property. Everybody but me, that is. In the aftermath of what we had experienced, the loud booms and bangs scared me half to death—but the many hugs and smiles, oohs and aahs as the fireworks lit up the sky, warmed my heart.

Most of the volunteers pulled out the next day. The departures were bittersweet for me. The house had been bustling with activity from the moment we returned from Gatlinburg, but now, as the travel trailers and motor homes pulled away, I felt a sadness wrap around me. I had been basking in so much support and encouragement. From now on, it would be just the kids and me, with the help of Tommy's parents nearby and, on occasion, my mom.

Several people who had worked on the project, including James and Marcy, stayed to attend church services with our family on Sunday morning. We all had so much for which we wanted to praise God.

Later that day, James set up a video camera on a tripod and did an interview with me, sort of wrapping up a collection of my thoughts about what we had experienced.

I felt so awkward talking about recent events, but I wanted to express our thanks to all the volunteers who had worked so hard on the project, as well as those who had contributed financial resources to help renovate our home. James made the process easier by asking questions, but I was still intimidated and uncomfortable on camera. We talked for thirty or forty minutes.

James made a closing video from the renovated living area. In it, he said, "Several weeks ago on the website, I posted a statement that said, 'I can't; you can't; but together, *we* can.'

"The family came home last night at seven p.m., and we were ready. Aw, there were a few touch-ups to be done here and there, but 99 percent of this house was completed in six days.

"I want to thank all the volunteers; the more than thirty-eight businesses in this area that came together to make this happen; the donors—many of whom did not even know this family.

"It was an incredible experience. I'll cherish it for the rest of my life and take it to my grave. It was my first [home makeover] experience, but it may not be my last.

"So for now, see you later, Lawrenceburg.

"And Schankweiler family, I hope you enjoy this house for many years to come. We sure did enjoy it for six days."

Before the Crockers left on Monday, James checked over the renovation one more time and found a minor problem with the septic system. He decided to fix it while he and Marcy were still there, so he invited Bubba to go with him to the nearby Home Depot store.

Bubba did not know James well, but he was aware that James had spearheaded Project Fresh Start and that he and Marcy had been so good to our family. Bubba rode along with James, and on the way, they had a poignant conversation.

"I'm so proud of you, son," James said. "You don't have to talk about anything, but if you need to talk, I'll be here for you. Are you traumatized?"

Bubba shook his head slightly. "No, I'm okay," he said, but offered no details. "I loved my dad, but he had turned into a monster. I knew what I had to do that day, and God gave me a peace. He gave me the courage."

James looked at Bubba in amazement.

Bubba continued, "I knew I'd probably spend the rest of my life in prison, but it didn't matter. I also knew that if I didn't kill Dad, he would kill our entire family."

James shook his head. "Ever since I heard what had happened," he said, "every time I see the word *courage*, I think of one person… and that's you."

They rode the rest of the way in relative silence, but the conversation left an indelible impression on James.

To make sure the septic system was functioning correctly, James and Marcy decided to stay one more day. I invited their daughter, Charlee, to stay with us. In an attempt to get life back to normal, I had planned to take Timmy and the girls to the annual fishing derby—a Lawrence County tradition in which the community stocked the pond so kids were almost guaranteed to catch some fish. We had to get up at four a.m. to get to the pond for the event, so I invited Charlee to sleep in my room.

Charlee slept between Tayler and me, and when I awakened her the next morning before daylight, I asked, "Do you want to go fishing?"

"Yeah!" she said with excitement in her little voice. The kids had a blast at the derby, and I was amazed at how quickly Charlee had bonded with our family.

As Marcy, James, and Charlee prepared to leave for Florida the following day, I stood by the front door and embraced them in long hugs. They had grown so special to my family and me. All too soon, they got in their green pickup truck and pulled out of the driveway. They were the last to roll out; all the campers and travel trailers were gone, and so was everybody else. It was a weird feeling. I felt so thankful, yet so alone.

When we approached the start of the next school year, the first semester following the incident, Bubba told me, "Mom, I don't think I want to go back to school after all the publicity." He was able to graduate, however, because his schoolteachers brought his homework to our house. He had homeschooled previously, so he was comfortable with that routine. His teachers helped tutor him and gave him his academic tests at our home. He graduated early from Lawrence County High School, but he didn't want to participate in the public graduation ceremonies.

Instead, he wanted to join the US Army. That was a tall order given the charges he had faced, and the probation on which he remained after he was released. It took some time for Bubba to be accepted by the military, but on March 4, 2011, almost three years since the day he had shot his abusive dad, I watched proudly as Bubba graduated from the army's infantry division in Fort Benning, Georgia. He would go on to serve six years in the US Army before being honorably discharged.

CHAPTER 39

The Return of the
Gregarious Groomsman

As life calmed down a bit, I recalled that within days after Tommy's funeral, as my mom had prepared to leave, she had stood in front of me in my kitchen and lovingly held my face in her hands. She looked into my eyes and innocently suggested, "Someday you're going to find love again, sweetie." At the time, I was too numb to even consider such an idea and told her so. I yanked her hands down. "Don't even say such a thing, Mom," I said sadly. Even as time went by, I did not anticipate a romantic relationship. Far from it.

Following Tommy's death, I lived as a single mom for the next seven years. During that time, I focused on each of my children. The kids and I powered through the transition period and made all sorts of good memories. Beyond that, I worked long hours at the rehabilitation center while studying hard to earn my registered nursing degree.

I had always planned to move back to Florida after my daughter, Tonie Jo, finished high school. She loved her classmates

269

and her school in Tennessee, so I felt it was important for her to graduate with the same group of friends with whom she had grown so close during her high school years. Tonie Jo made me promise we'd stay in Lawrenceburg till she got her high school diploma.

"Okay," I quipped, "I'll honor that request, but don't be surprised if I show up at your graduation ceremony driving a U-Haul!"

Tonie Jo laughed. She knew I was still a Florida girl at heart and that I was longing to return home. When we finally moved in 2014, it was bittersweet. We had experienced so much life—and death—with the good people of Lawrenceburg, so the boys elected to remain in Tennessee while the girls and I headed south.

And oddly enough, I also felt another pull drawing me to Florida.

I had talked to the Crockers almost daily after the renovation of our home was completed. There were still touch-ups to be done, items on back order, or other details I needed to know about. Months went by and we stayed in touch. Normally I talked with Marcy, but on several occasions when I called, Marcy wasn't home. Two or three times, James answered the phone instead. I thought that was odd, but nobody knew the renovation project better than James, so I was glad for his assistance.

After the third call in a row that Marcy did not answer, James admitted to me, "Well, we separated," which I found completely mind-blowing. They had worked so hard together and, seemingly, so well. On several occasions, I had noticed something odd about their relationship—but no indication their marriage was in trouble.

Over the next few months, James called occasionally, and I enjoyed talking with him. By then it was clear he and Marcy would divorce, and he explained the demise of their relationship without rancor or blame. They were both better off as friends rather than as marriage partners, he said.

The friendship between James and me deepened with time, and we talked more openly about what we had expected going into our marriages versus what we had actually experienced. Our phone calls grew longer and more frequent. Eventually, we struck up a long-distance dating relationship. I had not dated anyone at all since Tommy's death, so simply going out for an enjoyable evening was a refreshing experience for me. I felt comfortable with James and free to be myself. He was the man who had rescued me with no ulterior motives, so I had confidence in him.

Previously, I had been "living," but James showed me how to truly be alive. He challenged me to broaden my boundaries and invited me to try new experiences. He brought color into my black-and-white world. After years of my trying to blend in, James convinced me to stand out. He applauded me when I succeeded and helpfully critiqued me when I failed. His energy to accomplish his goals stretched my way of thinking. His transparent integrity and honesty helped heal my broken trust.

Not that our relationship was all honey and no bees. Quite the contrary. James and I went back and forth sporadically, our relationship moving one step forward and two steps back, sometimes passionately hot and sometimes icy cold. We broke up several times because we simply didn't think we could deal with all the baggage we both carried.

But during the times we were estranged, we missed each other terribly. There was an incompleteness to our lives. We knew we were better and stronger together.

Seven years after James and his volunteers renovated our home, James asked me to marry him—and I said, "Yes!"

A gifted limerick composer, James wrote a special piece for me. In it, he expressed the desire of his heart:

> I want your goods, and I'll take your bads;
> I want your lasses, and I want your lads.
> I'll take you on up days and on the downs too,
> I'll take all of whatever is you.
> I'll take you rich, and I'll take you poor.
> You leave me always wanting more.
> More of you, that is; I'm done with all others;
> You're at the top of my list of "druthers."
> I'll take you wet; I'll take you dry;
> I'll take your lows and take your highs.
> Forever with you is all I want.
> You're at the end of my lifelong hunt.
> For love, for life, for all that can be,
> Would you agree to do forever with me?
> Not next week, not next year;
> Not even tomorrow; right now, right here.
> Let's not waste another minute alone;
> Let's build a life; let's build a home.
> I know that much of the magic is gone,
> But the stage is still there that we made it on.
> We made magic before; we can make it again.
> To our sweet love, there will be no end.
> Even when age and death take their toll,
> They cannot touch what I feel in my soul.
> Make me the happiest man in the world,
> And agree to be my forever girl![1]

I looked at him and asked one question: "When?"

"Tomorrow," James replied. "I don't want to wait another day. Let's get married tomorrow."

On September 17, 2015, James and I were married in a simple ceremony under the gazebo at a local Florida courthouse. These days I sometimes quip that "James has been in both of my weddings!"

James had promised me for several years that he would show me the world. I knew he traveled for his business to various exotic locations, but James surprised me and wasted no time getting started. Shortly after we said, "I do," we took off for Dubai, Bali, Indonesia, and then India. In the years to follow, he took me to Israel, Egypt, and China, and we've traveled to numerous beautiful places since then.

James kept this promise and so many others he made to me. He truly exposed me to a whole new world, and more importantly, to a new way to live as a Christian couple. He opened up and shared his heart with me, both his worst faults and his greatest dreams and goals. He accepted me and loved me at my best and at my worst, always encouraging me to look to Jesus as our strength.

In a matter of utmost importance to me, James embraced my children—and they looked to him for fatherly advice and leadership. Sealing his commitment on October 19, 2022, James adopted my adult daughters, who had been so young when the horrible events had occurred in 2008. In his relationship with them, he modeled our heavenly Father, and in many ways he became the kind of father they never knew.

Bubba remained in Tennessee, where he married Cassie, a young woman from Lawrenceburg, in 2019. About a year later, they moved to Florida, where James employed Bubba in his business, Hog Technologies. He also employed Timothy that same year.

Similar to the Old Testament love story of Ruth and Boaz, James became my Boaz, picking up the pieces of our family and helping to put us all back together again.

These days, I often have to pinch myself to make sure I am not dreaming. *How do I wake up every morning to this new and wonderful life?* I wonder in amazement. I have a husband who loves me, respects me, and treats me with tenderness, and does so for my children as well. Bubba, Timothy, Tonie Jo, and Tayler are all grown-up now and on their own. It hasn't always been easy for them, and they haven't always made the best choices, yet I know our heavenly Father has them in His hand and has good things ahead for each of them.

I'm reminded of the biblical record of Solomon, king of Israel. God told Solomon he could ask for anything, but because Solomon asked God for wisdom rather than mere riches, power, or prestige, God honored Solomon and granted him all of that and more!

For years, my prayer was so simple: "God, please rescue us." That's all I asked, nothing else. Although I could never have imagined the circumstances through which that rescue would come, God answered my prayer and gave us so much more.

I am thriving; I am loved and cherished by the man I love and cherish. James truly is my knight in shining armor, and I am blessed and highly favored to be his wife.

CHAPTER 40

Speaking Out at Last

I know that not every person who has suffered at the hands of an abuser will have a triumphant story to tell. Many feel trapped and continue to endure suffering. Some will not live to tell about it. But my prayer is, by telling my story, others will find the hope and courage they need to get out of an abusive relationship.

For many years, I was reluctant to let anyone know about the abuse I suffered at my former husband's hands. I was embarrassed and self-conscious about it any time the subject came up, whether it pertained specifically to me or not. And I certainly did not want to mention the abuse in front of my children. They had lived through it and had barely survived. Why would I want to remind them of those horrendous experiences?

But increasingly, God nudged me, saying it was time to tell my story. When James and I attended a weekend conference featuring the popular author and leadership instructor John Maxwell, the Lord spoke to me through the speaker. In one of his sessions, Maxwell looked directly at me and said, "Write your story."

Today, I am determined to use my pain to help others avoid something similar in their lives. I now know many women have experienced abusive situations similar to what I endured with Tommy. One in three women report having experienced severe physical violence from an intimate partner in their lifetime.[2] Think of that: If you have a mom, a sister, a daughter, an aunt, or a female cousin, the horrible odds are that one of those women will suffer abuse. Today, my "older self" would insist that my younger self get out of that relationship the first time Tommy scared me and hit me. Especially before our children were born, it would have been much less complicated to have sought help from my family or simply to have moved away. Today, I warn women (and men) in abusive situations: Get out, get help now, while you can. To do anything less is to put your life, and the lives of your children, at greater risk every hour you remain in that relationship.

If you are unmarried and in a relationship with someone who speaks or acts abusively toward you, leave! Get out of that relationship. Don't assume a marriage will improve your odds of the abuser behaving better. That rarely happens. Unfortunately, the opposite occurs all too frequently. If he or she is abusing you *before* you marry, that abuse will only intensify *after* you marry.

The signs of partner abuse are not always easy to detect. Bruises or discolored skin around the eyes are not the only signals. As a nurse, I go through domestic violence training every two years so I can better discern the signs of trouble. But even after all I have endured and all I have studied, emotional and physical manipulation is still sometimes difficult to determine because the abused person may appear "normal."

In 2021 I was invited to serve on the board of directors of SafeSpace, a Florida-based organization and certified emergency shelter providing help to victims of intimate partner violence. There is no quick fix for the problem of domestic violence, but organizations like SafeSpace offer the protection individuals need when fleeing an abusive partner. I never knew places like this existed.

Through my work with this group, I've encountered numerous people that others would never guess have lived through abuse—but they have. Some have endured torturous relationships for years.

I accompanied James to a business trade show recently, and while sitting in a booth at the show, I struck up a conversation with a beautiful woman. As we talked, she opened up and said, "I was in an abusive relationship," and she began to share some details of what she had endured from her previous boyfriend. From the looks of her—seeing the way she dressed and presented herself, and knowing the family from which she came—few people would ever guess the torment she had been through. Abuse happens, and unfortunately, it can happen to any of us. It knows no socioeconomic boundaries.

Granted, many people don't talk about it because there is a lot of shame that comes along with partner abuse. A lot of judgment can come with it too. I know this to be true, and I'm sensitive to it in others—so I never push too hard to get someone to tell me his or her story.

Even by talking about my own story, I make myself vulnerable all over again every time I recount the details—details I kept deeply hidden for years. I've seen the responses in the faces of audiences; even if they aren't verbally asking the questions, they're thinking, *Why in the world would you stay with such a monster? Why would you do that to yourself? Why would you put your kids through that?*

So when I try to explain, I am aware that some people will judge me without understanding all the facts—and that is not a fun place to be. But I know it is important to tell the story anyway, to shine a light in the darkness. I understand all too well that abuse is happening to many people around us. I know that women who have been through it, or who are going through it, need somebody who understands, someone with whom they can identify, who can feel their pain and help them get out of those awful situations.

So I muster my courage and tell my story, letting people know what can happen in the blink of a black eye.

But it is vital to understand: When you come against partner abuse, it is not simply a temperamental spouse, personal anger, or societal ignorance you are confronting. You are entering a real spiritual battle in which the Enemy has his hands around somebody's neck. This territory has been held by demonic forces for years, and if you are going to confront that, you must prepare yourself spiritually and trust in the power of God—not your own intelligence, persuasiveness, or physical ability.

Moreover, it is not a once-and-done sort of battle; it is perpetual. The Enemy does not give up his territory easily and will continually launch counterattacks, attempting to reclaim anything he has lost. He searches for any opening in your protection, and he is quick to hit you in your most sensitive spots when you are already burdened with embarrassment, guilt, misunderstanding, fear, or the desire to protect your children.

Today, I am more than sixteen years on the other side of my abusive relationship with Tommy, and I still deal with some horrific memories. James has to gently nudge me awake in the middle of the night on occasion, saying, "Wake up, babe, you're having a nightmare," as unspeakable scenes replay on the movie screen of my mind.

Beyond that, my kids have all faced serious emotional challenges and struggles as a result of what they witnessed in our home. It has not been easy, and it has not always been pretty. I pray for them daily, that God will help them overcome any negative memories they carry stemming from my abusive marriage.

Partner abuse never simply goes away; it is never done with the bruises, and only Jesus can heal your broken spirit.

My message is strong and straightforward: If you're in an abusive relationship, get out *now*. But get out safely with the help of law enforcement and organizations such as SafeSpace. I know it's scary, and I understand that you're terrified to make that move, because in many cases, it could be the most dangerous move of your life. But if you take that step, you're getting away not only from the imminent danger—every day I woke up and thought, *Will this be my last day on earth? Will my kids find me dead?*—but also from future harm to yourself and your children as well. The stuff you leave behind is replaceable; the clothes, couches, refrigerator, furniture, televisions, cars, or trucks... They can all be replaced. What is not replaceable is *you*—and the lives of your children. That's why it is imperative to get out safely.

I wish it was just me carrying this heavy load for the rest of my life. That's awful enough. But because I did *not* get out when I might have, my four adult children now carry heavy burdens in their hearts and minds as well.

Yes, I'm thankful to God that He redeems us. He bought us back through Jesus's death on the cross. But I wish I had not permitted my fears to reap a negative harvest in my children. My daily prayer for my kids is not so much that God would erase their memories of their childhood, but that God will use those memories in their futures—that He will keep the good He can use from their pasts and erase the unprofitable pain they feel on a daily basis.

Not a day goes by that I am not affected by the abuse I suffered, in some form or fashion. And I have to pray it out of my head. I have to stop and remind myself, *Okay, this is not what I need to be thinking about.* But for the value I can bring to SafeSpace and to other victims of abuse, I am willing to use it.

Whenever I speak on the subject of domestic violence or tell my own story, I must fortify myself spiritually. The devil is lurking nearby any time I dredge up the horrific memories from my past, and he is constantly ready to drag me down if possible. So I've learned how to strengthen myself by filling my mind with God's Word, by flooding my heart with praises for our mighty God and who He is. As such, I put on the full armor of God as described in Ephesians 6. I don't want to give the devil an opportunity to get back into my thoughts, my heart, or my subconscious mind.

Even when James and I are watching television, I need to be careful. We don't usually plan to watch programs about domestic violence, but many of the informational shows nowadays will deal with abuse issues. That's good news and bad: good because the public is becoming more aware; bad because those shows can depict situations that trigger horrible memories for me, and in an instant, I am right back "there"—experiencing the horrendous abuse again.

Certain songs or movies can also remind me of things I endured, so I need to counter their effects in my spirit. Sometimes I simply need to turn off the television, or better yet, change the channel and let something good into my mind. Scripture says, "Be anxious for nothing, but in everything by prayer and supplication with thanksgiving let your requests be made known to God. And the peace of God, which surpasses all comprehension, will guard your hearts and your minds in Christ Jesus. Finally, brethren, whatever is true, whatever is honorable, whatever is right, whatever is pure, whatever is lovely, whatever is of good repute, if there is any excellence and if anything worthy of praise, dwell on these things" (Philippians 4:6–8 NASB 1995). Despite the memories that sometimes remind me of the abuse I suffered, I choose to ponder the goodness of God.

For years I lived on "Someday Isle": Someday I'll escape from this abusive prison. Someday my children will be safe. Someday I will no longer live in fear. Someday I'll have a better life. Perhaps, had I stepped out in faith and trusted God to take care of my children and me, someday could have come sooner. I'll never know.

On the other hand, one of the great temptations of life is to make someday *today*—by attempting to manipulate events in *my* time, in *my* way, rather than God's. I had to learn to trust God for the good things He had in store for me, which required patience and faith. But God *is* faithful, and He did not disappoint me. We often think, hope, and even pray that "someday my prince will come." Mine did! I know God will provide for you as well.

ACKNOWLEDGMENTS

Special thanks to Attorney Daniel Freeman. When I decided to write this book, I contacted Mr. Freeman and asked him if he had kept any files from Bubba's case.

He said, "It's interesting that you called. I'm about to retire, and I told my assistant that we could destroy any files dating back beyond ten years. So I will be happy to return all that I have to you."

Thanks to Attorney Freeman, in addition to my own recollections, I have been able to rely on his contemporaneous notes from our initial meetings regarding what happened that fateful Good Friday. I am forever indebted to him.

To Tommy (Bubba), Timmy, Tonie Jo, and Tayler, I hope this book can help you sort out the memories from your past that might be blurred due to your young age or buried deep within due to trauma. May it help answer questions you might have had but never asked. May it also offer insight into why I felt forced to stay in the dangerous dysfunction in which we lived.

No words can accurately describe how badly I feel for the emotional and physical pain you each endured, including what you saw and heard over the years. For that, I'm sorry.

I pray God will protect your mind and heart as you read, realizing this book contains dramatic details of accounts you have probably chosen to forget.

I also tried to forget, but it was only after I forced myself to remember that I gained control of these memories and no longer allowed them to control me. With God's help, I have safely put them behind me where they belong, and hope you can do the same.

To my husband, James. Thank you for being the loudest voice in my ear encouraging me to tell my story. Because of your support, I found the courage to face my past. You challenged me to rethink my reasons for not writing and when I said, "What if it hurts," you responded, "What if it helps?"

You saw something in me that I could not, and now I am stronger for it. Thank you for giving me all the "space" I needed to remember, research, and write. You have not only shown me a whole new life, but you've shown me a whole new way to live... which is "courageously." Thank you for leading by example.

To my writer, Ken Abraham. Thank you for believing in me and for convincing me that my story mattered. You sifted through hundreds of my tangled-up words, straightened them out, and made them make sense. You patiently helped me share painful accounts with sensitivity and accuracy. Although some of the information I shared was deeply personal, I never felt judged or embarrassed. Your patience and professionalism throughout this process never wavered. I am blessed to have learned from such a gifted writer.

RESOURCES

Common lies victims of abuse believe

"Nobody will believe me."

"I could never make it on my own."

"Nobody will love me after what I have been through."

"Having children will improve our relationship."

"If I give him/her another chance, he/she will change for the better."

"If I leave, nobody will be there to help me."

"If I tell anyone about the abuse, I will regret it."

"Everyone has a bad day now and then..."

Where to find help if you are in an abusive relationship:

National Domestic Violence Hotline:	1-800-799-7233
Blue Monarch bluemonarch.org:	931-924-8900
Christian Broadcasting Network Helpline:	1-800-700-7000
Association of Christian Counselors:	1-800-526-8673
SafeSpace info@safespacefl.org:	772-223-2399.

How you can help:

- Understand that the problem exists, that it is complicated, and that it has no quick fix.
- Be proactive. If you see something that raises your suspicions, be willing to say something.

- Build a relationship with the person about whom you are concerned.
- Be courageous enough to express your concern without judgment and to tactfully speak up when you see bruises or other evidence of abuse.
- Be aware of available resources where an abused person can find help.
- Support organizations that are helping victims of abuse.

Endnotes

1 James Crocker, © September 16, 2015.
2 Centers for Disease Control and Prevention, "Fast Facts: Preventing Intimate Partner Violence," accessed January 29, 2024, https:/www.cdc.gov/ violenceprevention/intimatepartnerviolence/fastfact.html.